Everything I Know about Life I Learned from PowerPoint

Russell Davies has squandered what talents he has learning more about PowerPoint, creativity and communication than is really healthy. He's used PowerPoint inside 10 Downing Street, written about it for *Wired*, and put it in a MoMA exhibition. And along the way, he has PowerPointed for organisations like Nike, Microsoft and Apple.

Everything I Know about Life I Learned from PowerPoint

and Keynote and Slides and Prezi and all the rest

Russell Davies

PROFILE BOOKS

First published in Great Britain in 2021 by
Profile Books Ltd
29 Cloth Fair
London
EC1A 7JQ

www.profilebooks.co.uk

1 3 5 7 9 10 8 6 4 2

Printed and bound in China by 1010
Printing International Ltd.

A CIP catalogue record for this book is available from the British Library.

ISBN 978 1 78816 737 6
eISBN 978 1 78816 736 9

MIX
Paper from responsible sources
FSC® C016973

Mark Zuckerberg, billionaire founder of Facebook, gets so nervous and sweaty before a presentation that he has his assistant blow-dry his armpits.

This is a book about not having to do that.

It's what I've learned from thirty years of PowerPoint about how to communicate, be creative and not get too scared.

It's all dead simple.

There's nothing about changing the way you stand or learning to breathe through your feet. It's just about leaning on PowerPoint and using it a little bit better.

If you're looking for all the easy jokes about PowerPoint, you've come to the wrong place. I'm going for the hard jokes. The ones showing how good, positive and democratising it is. I am here to praise it, not bury it.

PowerPoint seems to be the software we hate to love. Everyone uses it because it's so useful, creative and interesting, yet the popular perception is all 'Death by PowerPoint' and clip-art memes. Well, this ain't that. This is a celebration. Get your clicker and prepare to party.

Next slide please.

Don't @ me

PowerPoint is not the only fruit

Some places in this book I'm talking specifically about the software package invented by Robert Gaskins and his team and sold by Microsoft. Especially when we're looking at the history and development of the thing. But most of the time I'm using PowerPoint to stand in for Presentation Software – the category it created. (I imagine Microsoft's lawyers will hate that. They'll be as angry as when people use Hoover to mean 'vacuum cleaner' or Google to mean 'abuse of monopoly power'.) So, if you're a fan of Keynote or Slides or LibreOffice or Pitch or Prezi, yes I'm talking about your thing too. Except Prezi.*

More a way of life

This is not a definitive history – though someone should write that, I would read the hell out of it. And it's not a comprehensive How To either. It's more of a scrapbook, or, if you're being fancy, a commonplace book. PowerPoint is a fantastic way to collect things and to rub ideas together, so a lot of what you've got in here is that. Interesting bits and bobs about PowerPoint, its creation, its success and how it gets used. If you want the best history you should read *Sweating Bullets* by Robert Gaskins. If you want the best How To go for *slide:ology* by Nancy Duarte.

Yes, this should really have been a presentation

You're right. What can I say? But it's a book. Let's just try to move on.

Tip One: Leave stuff out

There's a lot of advice in this book about all the things you can put in your presentations. I also bang on a lot about keeping them short and focused. This is unhelpfully contradictory. So here's a useful tip: start with a list of all the things you're not going to cover.

* I'm joking, I'm joking. I love you Prezi people.

When you prepare a presentation you do a lot of homework and research and thinking. It's natural to get attached to that stuff. You want to demonstrate the effort you've made. And to make it clear that you've thought about the edge cases and the extra things people might ask about. If you do all that, though, you'll overwhelm your main point with detail, so just start by saying: this is what we're going to cover and this is what we're not. People will stop wondering when you're going to talk about their pet issue.

And so this is what I'm not going to cover. It's all fascinating but I had to leave stuff out.

PowerPoint and comedy, PowerPoint in schools, PowerPoint in churches, the differences between all the different presentation tools, what the best animations and transitions are (none of them), how to pitch for VC money, the Netflix 'culture deck', slideshare, why academic PowerPoint is so bad, all the various presentation tools written in HTML5, PowerPoint karaoke, PechaKucha, aspect ratio, the multiscreen installations of Charles and Ray Eames, 2 × 2 grids. And that thing you deeply care about? I thought about that but had to leave it out. For secret reasons.

I've also not written much about PowerPoint in the time of coronavirus. I began this book just as the first UK lockdown started and finished it as we were emerging from the last one. Hopefully. So it's inflected with virus. And there was a lot of PowerPoint about during the pandemic. My parents are in their eighties, for instance, and watching the government briefings on the telly was the first time they'd ever seen it. I could have focused obsessively on the design of those slides. And on the strange choice to keep saying 'next slide please' instead of giving Chris Whitty a clicker. But, frankly, it feels too recent and raw. I talk a bit about those briefings but not in the detail you might want.

Similarly, many of us have spent the last year experiencing a crash course in presenting via Zoom or Teams or whatever Google are calling their version this week. That has not been easy and there are obviously lessons to be learned. But I don't think we've learned them yet, so that'll have to wait for the paperback.

Contents

PART ONE

PowerPoint Saved My Life

I'm very shy. Embarrassingly, selfishly shy. I hate meeting new people or being in unstructured social settings like parties, lunches or, well, most of modern life outside a monastery.

The only serious arguments my wife and I have ever had have been about my extreme reluctance to attend weddings where you have to sit next to people you don't know.

And yet I love working in the kinds of creative industries where all these things are virtually compulsory. You have to meet, share your work, talk about your ideas and present to strangers all the time. I always wanted to work in that kind of world. I was terrified I wouldn't be able to.

I found the answer early on – PowerPoint.

With PowerPoint by my side I realised that being on stage and presenting ideas was something I enjoyed and could get good at.

You've escaped the randomness of people and put yourself in control. You're doing a presentation. You're in charge. You can avoid the embarrassment and terror by simply being well prepared. More prepared than anyone in the history of the world ever.

And so I've defeated that shyness and been blessed with a very fortunate career.

I've helped make advertising for Nike, Honda and Microsoft. I've consulted for organisations from Apple to Unilever. I've made 'PowerPoint artefacts' that ended up in New York's Museum of Modern Art. And I've paid some of the spiritual debt for all that relentless capitalism by helping the UK government build better websites and persuade a million people to switch to renewable energy.

I've done presentations all around the world and in places no one's ever presented before.

Most of that work has been as a 'Creative Strategist' – one of those awful titles that makes me sound like one of the worst people in the world. In advertising they call it 'Account Planning'. In other industries it's called 'Communications Strategy'. I never go to stand-up shows for fear that I'll be forced on to the front row and I'll have to shout out my occupation for ritualised comedic abuse.

My job normally involves thinking about how an organisation should present itself to people. How do we get our message across? How do we explain things well? So I've spent a lot of time thinking about how communication works and why people do, or don't, pay attention to what you're saying.

Although you might well have seen some of the work I've been involved with – Nike ads, those famous Honda ones, GOV.UK – you won't have seen the PowerPoint that led to them. Given it's so ubiquitous, PowerPoint is oddly private. It doesn't make it into the mass media much. It's shared in closed rooms, not public channels. It's telling that quite a few of the examples I provide in this book only emerged through court cases and subpoenas. PowerPoint is often built out of copyrighted material: other people's images, thoughts and ideas. That's part of its strength but it's also a reason it doesn't get out much. (And it's been one of the challenges of producing this book. Come and watch me do a presentation version and you'll see all the illicit PowerPoint goodies we weren't allowed to use.)

And, although it was designed as a tool for presentation, it's increasingly become a tool for archiving and thinking. I know I'm not alone in having hard drives full of PowerPoint. Thirty years of it. All of it accessible and readable on a modern computer because Microsoft have done such a good job of making it backwards compatible. They know that all human knowledge is now stored in PowerPoint. And I'm also not alone in having a lifetime of ideas, inspirations, tricks and techniques boiled down into slides. PowerPoint has become a container for my ideas, a useful way of looking at and understanding the world and a brilliant way of playing around with those ideas.

So this book is a place where I can share my enthusiasm for the extraordinary ways in which PowerPoint has taken over the world. It's my opportunity to tell you some of the magic behind it. How it came to be. Why it is the way it is, why that works and why you should know about Robert Gaskins. It's also a scrapbook of all the things I've learned about presentations and presenting and, more broadly, creativity, communications and attention.

A friend of mine once told me that my theories of how to do a presentation seemed pretty much like my theories of how to build a brand – stick together a loose accumulation of interesting, vaguely related stuff and it'll be much more compelling than anything pre-planned and rigid. He was right. That's the plan with this book too.

So here's a vaguely related quote from Haruki Murakami's *What I Talk About When I Talk About Running*:

> Somerset Maugham once wrote that in each shave lies a philosophy. I couldn't agree more. No matter how mundane some action might appear, keep at it long enough and it becomes a contemplative, even meditative act.

There's nothing more mundane than PowerPoint. And I've kept at it for thirty years. Bring on the meditations.

Before presentations

Until I got to university I assumed I wanted to be a writer. I was reasonably good at it as a child. I liked reading books. (Sort of, not as much as watching telly or listening to music, but more than visiting stately homes or cold-water swimming.)* My dream career, combining some of my interests, would have been reviewing TV for a newspaper.

When I got to university I realised I wasn't going to be a writer because all the people I met there were going to do that ahead of me. And their parents already did it or knew someone who did it. Or they had spent the summer doing it. Or already had their own column. Or just radiated writerly confidence, knew what 'parts of speech'

* Cold-water swimming was the only option available in the 1970s. You'd do it in a swimming pool. It was supposed to be heated, it just wasn't. It was the 1970s.

were and had done 'debate' at school. I was just the best at essays in my A-level English class at an unremarkable Midlands comprehensive.

The only alternative I could think of was advertising. Which I knew all about because I loved two TV programmes that featured it: *Bewitched* and *thirtysomething*. Assuming these to be fairly faithful and accurate depictions of the profession, I looked forward to something that blended creativity, commerce and cocktails, snappy language and clever ideas. Like poetry, but well paid.

The only dread spectre was the prospect of doing 'presentations'. They seemed important from the telly. There'd normally be a moment where someone would stand in front of clients with a flipchart or holding up some big white cards with ads on them and do a sales pitch, explaining what a genius idea it was. I couldn't imagine anything more horrific.

And yet advertising still appealed. I liked the implicit fuck you to the lazy assumptions about 'suitable careers' my university life had prepared me for. I also liked that they were going to pay me quite a lot. Margaret Thatcher had made it possible for students to get credit cards for the first time and I owed a lot of money on mine. I'd spent a fortune on overtly non-student clothes. I had issues.

So I ended up in advertising. Quietly worrying about the prospect of 'presentations' without knowing what they were.

It started with a trick

The first presentation I remember doing was early in my career in advertising at the tail end of the 1980s.

No one did PowerPoint in those days but as part of my junior advertising executive training I had been asked to prepare a presentation for my bosses. I was terrified.

I'd never done a presentation or anything like it – it wasn't a thing you did at school or university in

It's a kind of magic

Put two cards on a table and ask someone to pick one. If they pick the one you want then you've done it, boom, carry on. Declare victory.

If they pick the other one then just discard it and go, 'OK, so we're throwing that one away and that leaves us with this one.' You're now left with just the right card. Again, boom.

Do it quickly and breezily and no one will notice.

Well, little kids won't anyway.

those days, unless you joined some sort of weird dining society to practise speeches and train for a life in politics. I was so convinced it was going to be a disaster that I decided to make an extra-special effort that would distract from the fact that I was obviously an imposter.

I went to the library and got a book about magic tricks.

And then I started my presentation by saying that I had, in fact, prepared three presentations and that I was going to let the audience pick which one I'd do. I showed them three cards with three topics on, they picked one and, through some elaborate shenanigans, that was MIRACULOUSLY the one I had actually prepared for.

Even more miraculously the whole thing sort of worked. No one noticed that the content of the presentation was slightly shoddy, they were just charmed by the entertainment and the effort I'd put into the trick.

I felt the strange introverted thrill of being the centre of attention but also being in control. I was able to be with other people without finding it draining. Maybe presentations are for me, I thought.

The PowerPoint cometh

In those days we mostly did presentations on 'acetates' or 'overheads'. They were transparent bits of plastic, normally A4. You could print on them or write on them with a felt pen and you put them on a large, very bright projector which would beam the result on the wall.

You wouldn't use them for the whole presentation in the way we use PowerPoint, just when you were sharing diagrams or tables. That would normally be the strategy bit, the bit I'd do, so I wouldn't just have to stand there and emote – I had something to lean on.

The lights would have to be lowered so the projected image was visible; the curtains would be drawn. It was often a moment for our clients to take a nap. They were mostly waiting for the exciting bit – the ads. These were never shown on anything as low-fidelity or déclassé as overheads. They'd be carefully and expensively printed on huge bits of fancy shiny cardboard, carried around in enormous (and enormously pricey) black leather art bags. A big creative meeting would involve more cardboard than an Amazon warehouse wrapped in fancier luggage than went down with the *Titanic*.

But, at the time I was starting in advertising, computers were creeping into the workplace and PowerPoint was starting to show up in our clients' meetings.

I began to be intrigued by its possibilities. My job was to think about what we should communicate, and to whom, and why. And I had to persuade our

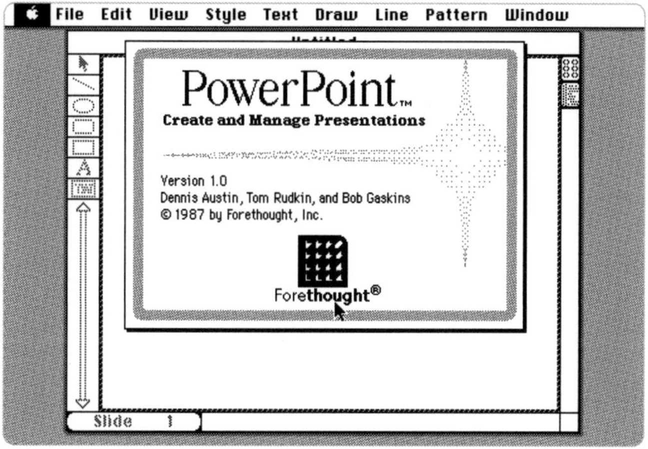

PowerPoint 1.0 – I don't think I ever used this version. Look! Dennis, Tom and Bob. You can read more about their adventures in Bob Gaskins' book.

clients that the ads we'd come up with were both dazzlingly creative and reassuringly effective. This meant doing big, set-piece presentations about the intersection of ideas, commerce, creativity and data. It seemed that a tool like PowerPoint was especially suited to that. And being good at PowerPoint might have some of the superficial, distracting benefits you get from starting your presentation with a magic trick. That also meant getting into computers. They were still a workplace rarity, and as it was now the early 1990s, that also meant getting into the internet.

Pretty soon I started wondering what the internet might mean for advertising, communications and creativity. Then people started organising conferences about that stuff, and since not many of us knew anything about it – it was a very fringe interest – I started speaking at them. I enjoyed it! And PowerPoint was a real help when you were on a big stage. So I dived further in and started to learn its ways.

Version 2.0 came along, for Windows, and then BANG! Version 3.0 for Macintosh.

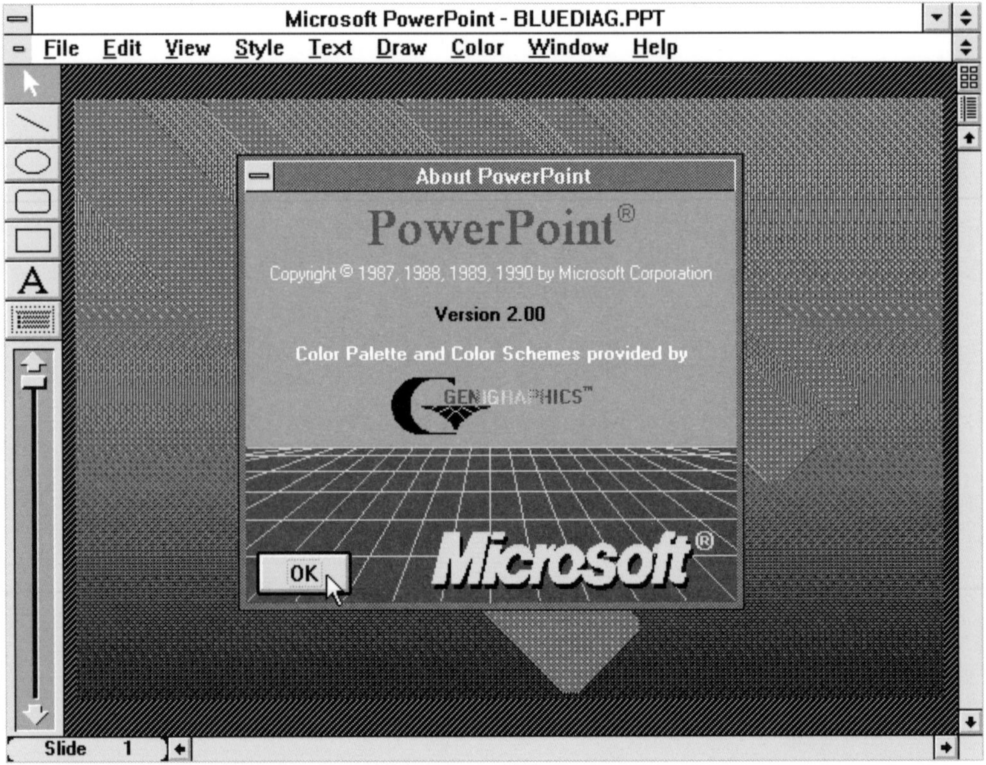

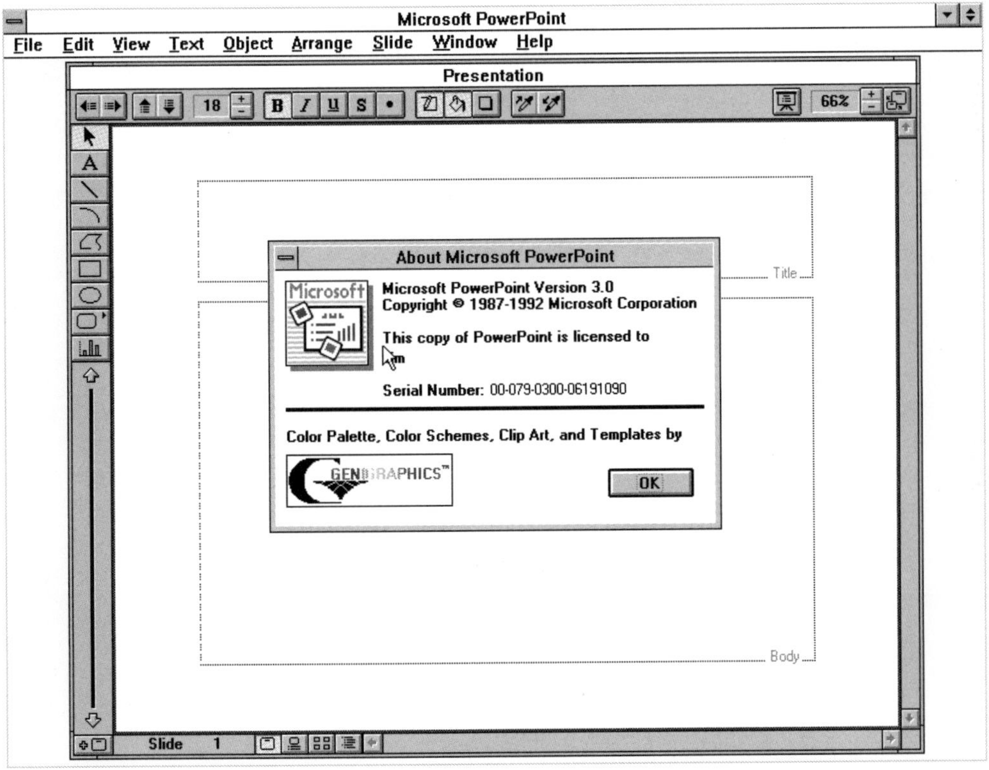
Microsoft PowerPoint
File
Edit
View
Text
Object
Arrange
Slide
Window
Help
Presentation
18
B
I
U
S
66%
About Microsoft PowerPoint
Microsoft
Microsoft PowerPoint Version 3.0
Copyright © 1987-1992 Microsoft Corporation
This copy of PowerPoint is licensed to
Serial Number: 00-079-0300-06191090
Color Palette, Color Schemes, Clip Art, and Templates by
GENIGRAPHICS™
OK
Title
Body
Slide 1

New tricks

And so I became the first person I knew who could put an image into a PowerPoint presentation.

This seems so banal now but at the time it was an absolute and extraordinary miracle. Getting an image on to a computer in the first place was quite a battle. Once you'd done that you'd have to convert it into a format PowerPoint could understand. Working that out could take, literally, days.

I would do presentations that included an image – a picture of my client's product – and people were bowled over. Clients were just so desperate to find out how to get an image into PowerPoint that they'd approve my strategies as an afterthought.

That was the entire basis of my career for quite a few years.

Just Doing It

Then, in 1996, my PowerPoint-derived enthusiasm for computers landed me my dream job.

I moved from mediocre advertising jobs in London to Portland, Oregon, and the best advertising agency in the world; a chaotic, fiercely creative and stubbornly independent bunch of artists and athletes called Wieden & Kennedy. They were famous for inventing 'Just Do It' and doing a ton of great advertising for Nike and others.

On the strength of that, they had just won all of Microsoft's advertising business and had drafted in a bunch of computer people to help bring all their magic creativity to bear on the resolutely un-magical world of PCs. This meant I was now dreamily close to the special source of the special sauce. I worked with the Office team. I met the Product Manager for PowerPoint!

(Strangely, even though I was fascinated by PowerPoint, even when I was travelling three times a week to the Microsoft campus, I didn't wonder anything at all about its origins. It simply didn't occur to me. I don't think people thought about that stuff back then. Software and consumer computing was too new for us to consider its origins. Now the inventors of the Mario Brothers or the Roland TR-808 drum machine are celebrated – back then no one thought to ask about them.)

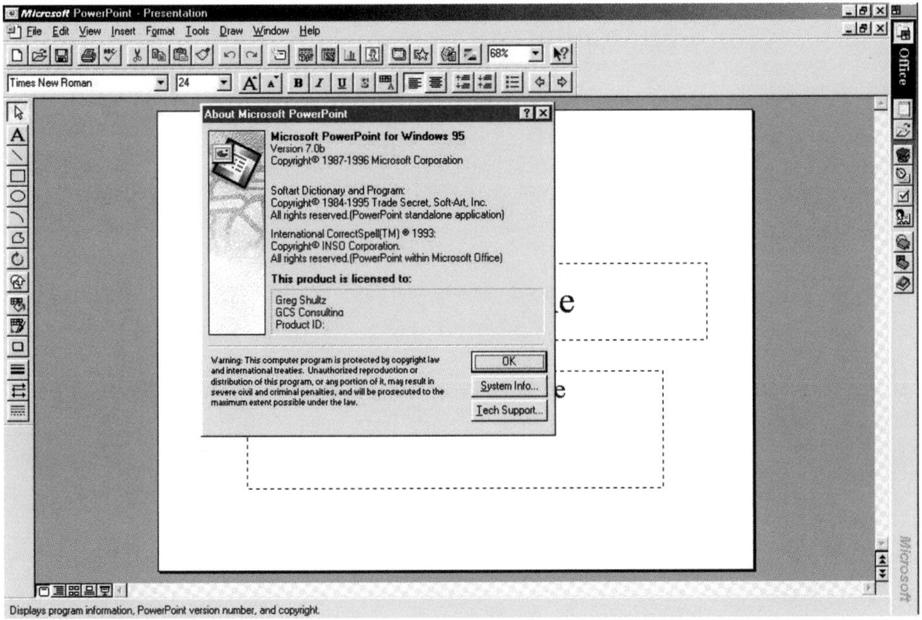

PowerPoint for Windows 95. Where I worked every day for about ten years.

The Tufte Club

I spent almost ten years at Wieden & Kennedy. Five in Portland and five back in London setting up a UK outpost. I learned from some of the best minds in creativity and communications. I worked on famous advertising campaigns for Nike and Coke. And non-famous ones for AltaVista and Stamps.com. And all those brilliant Honda ads. The one with the chain reaction of car parts, and that one with the animated bunnies.

They taught me to sweat the tiny details in writing, how one word here or there makes a real difference, how to bash a vague concept into a useful idea, how to work productively with the ambiguous, amorphous worlds of emotion and art.

They even paid for me to go to a day-long seminar given by a special, visionary man called Edward Tufte – one of the first people to think properly about how to present information. No one thought harder than Tufte about how it was received by an audience, about how much you had to work to make sure you were communicating what you intended.

I realised that this was deep, fertile territory. Presenting wasn't just something you did, it was something you could think about.

And Wieden & Kennedy was the perfect place to have this epiphany. Our presentations were as brilliant as our advertising. We regularly managed to make our clients cry, in a good way, often by reading them a poem. When I started there it was still 80 per cent cardboard and art bags; by the time I left it was 90 per cent PowerPoint. The software was maturing; it started to be something you could manipulate, almost as powerful as more 'creative' software like Photoshop. It was something you could play with. And we used its powers to invent a new kind of meeting – we combined performance, art, language, design and enormous words on a screen into a sort of elaborate business theatre. We learned how to perform with an image, how to change pace and direct attention. And, because it was still computers, how to always, always travel with a back-up presentation on paper.

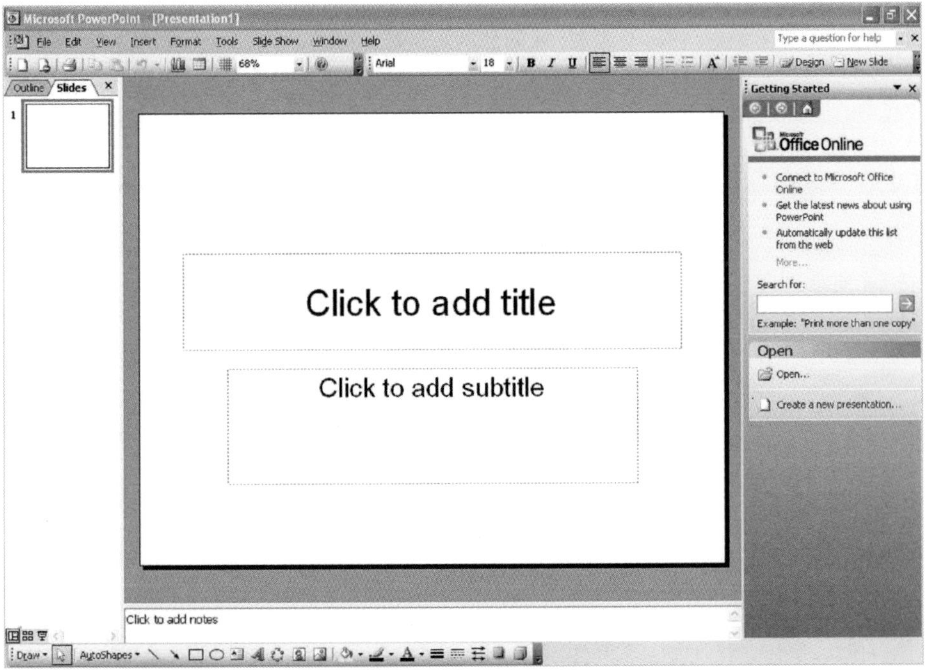

2003. PowerPoint was starting to get bloated and unwieldy. Powerful but with lots of menus and complications. Apple introduced Keynote in 2003 – people liked the relative simplicity.

TEDward

Fast-forward to 2006; another big moment. I had moved from W&K to working directly for Nike and they were good enough to pay for me to attend a rather unusual and esoteric thing called TED.

This was an exclusive, very expensive conference in Monterey, California. Which no one had heard of. Extraordinary speakers from the arts, sciences and literature gathered for three days and gave eighteen-minute talks to an attentive and enthusiastic audience high on ideas and VIP networking.

I hated the networking but I was bowled over by the format.

These were the presentations I'd been doing at work but transformed into a new format, a sort of intellectual entertainment. It was wholly fresh and original, not yet a cliché. A modern, multimedia, short-attention-span format but directed at a live audience.

It was like non-fiction theatre.

(Nowadays TED is something different. They've 'pivoted to video' and become about 'Ideas Worth Spreading'. Back then it was almost the opposite, more like 'You Had To Be There'. I understand why they made the change – it's admirably democratic and accessible to put everything online – but they lost something in the process. What made TED brilliant was that it was live – the presenters optimised their performance for the people in the room. Now they're structured and rehearsed for video and you lose a lot.)

I liked TED so much I started saving up to go back the following year. I'd quit Nike to go freelance by this point and moved back to London, so I was going to have to pay for myself. With the flights and everything else it was going to cost more than £5,000.

It suddenly occurred to me that I could just take that money and create my own version. A similar conference, but in London, handy for me. Everything I loved about TED (short presentations about interesting stuff) and none of what I hated (the expense, the networking, the sponsors).

Interesting and Boring

So the Interesting conferences were born. A series of days in unusual venues, with ordinary people doing short presentations about things they found interesting, all recruited via the internet. This was the heyday of personal blogging. You could follow a few links and find someone with a passion for something obscure but fascinating. They were delighted to come along and share that love in person and, almost universally, they turned out to be great presenters.

This taught me three things.

First, almost everyone can be a great presenter. You just need to talk about something you care or know about, and you need to do it to a supportive audience.

Second, there are lots of different ways to be great.

Very few of the best talks at Interesting felt anything like a TED talk or a typical corporate keynote. I didn't make anyone rehearse or send their presentation in advance. Nothing was very polished. People were hesitant, they stumbled over their words, they weren't always clear, they sometimes didn't make sense. But every Interesting was a joy. People were themselves and they connected. They weren't performing so much as just being slightly bigger versions of themselves on a stage, with PowerPoint (or often, by this time, Keynote) by their side as a helper and a prompt.

That was the third thing I learned: put as much of yourself into your presentation as you can. That's what connects. That's why people watch. Otherwise they may as well just read your notes.

Interesting conferences ended up happening all over the world. Organised by people who just fancied doing it.

I never made a penny from them but they were some of the best days of my life. They were an early part of a new world of 'intellectual leisure'. Other pioneers, in different forms and formats, were things like Ignite, Playful and the Do Lectures. And there was my favourite, a brilliant series of conferences called Boring. They were exactly the same as Interesting but with a much better name.

PowerPointless

Now that I was a freelancer I embarked on the rather esoteric and discombobulating practice of turning up at places – conferences, companies, corporate retreats – doing a presentation for forty minutes, and getting paid for it.

It always felt like I was getting away with something, like at any moment a small boy might pop out of the audience and shout, 'That man's got no ideas', but when I could dampen down the imposter syndrome it was fascinating work.

My talks would normally be some combination of work I'd done (Honda, Nike, internet stuff) and prognostications and advice about what that might mean for the future.

People seemed to enjoy it and find it valuable. They'd ask me to come back. I got to work with a huge range of fascinating organisations and I learned a lot about keeping an audience engaged and attentive. But after a while I began to notice that nothing was happening as a result of anything I said.

One year, for instance, I did a presentation for a big packaged goods company. They were keen to know how to make their advertising better and how they should be experimenting with digital projects. It seemed to go well. A couple of years later, they asked me to come back and do another presentation on exactly the same topic. It turned out they'd made absolutely no progress on anything I'd talked about. I did the previous presentation again but with all the recommendations dialled down to become even more achievable. A few years later they asked me back again. Same problem. Same results.

2007. I feel like this was when everyone had to start knowing what 'aspect ratio' meant.

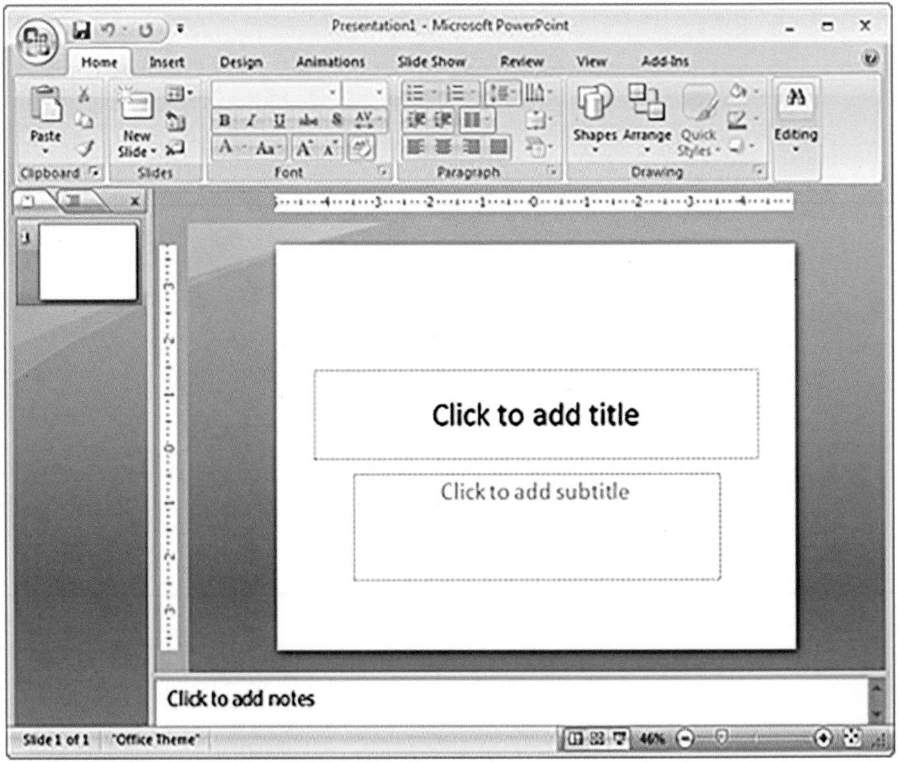

It finally dawned on me that I was just a corporate treat. An interesting moment out of the office but nothing to do with real work. This wasn't great. I felt like a fraud.

So I decided to start talking to the people rather than the companies. I'd take the same gigs but offer career thoughts rather than corporate ones. It was mostly simple stuff: pay attention to the internet, you might need to know about it for your job. (That was slightly more radical at the time. Especially if you worked for the sort of large organisation that could afford to hire me to waste one of your afternoons.) Quite a few people have told me they quit their jobs after one of my presentations. I think they meant it in a good way.

But the corporate bookers began to suspect something and I started getting fewer of those jobs. And then, when the financial crash hit, this work dried up altogether and I had to slink back to a corporate job in a big advertising agency. Fortunately it involved lots of training people how to do presentations, so I could continue to ride my little hobby horse.

And I was getting much better at it. When I was asked to speak at a conference I made sure I sat through all the other speakers so I could learn from what they did. It became clear how good presenters are very much like comedians. They make their presentation seem fresh and spontaneous but, what you're seeing has been crafted and honed through dozens, or hundreds, of performances. I was getting to the same point. I knew which bits worked, how to get a laugh and how to get people taking notes (give them a five-point list). I discovered a beginning that worked for me and I began to use it for every presentation I did. I'm still using it now. It's been almost ten years. About five years ago I found the perfect ending. Still using that as well.

And I started including more music and video in my presentations. I started inventing products and projects specifically to have something to talk about at conferences. I made a robot that recited poetry, a Twitter bot that wrote corporate slogans (@taglin3r) and I invented the Big Red Button, a huge red plastic button I could use to advance my slides. It was designed so conference organisers couldn't stop me taking my laptop on stage (they're obsessed with hiding the reality of how presentations happen) but it turned into a statement about performance and agency in presentations and ended up on display at the Museum of Modern Art in New York. I seemed to be making art about PowerPoint now.

All of which, combined with my relentless blogging about the presentations I was doing, meant people started to realise I was one of the few people in the world who was actively interested in PowerPoint. It became a thing people knew about me. Like your uncle who collects pottery owls. So they started sending me articles and news stories about it and journalists started asking me to comment on it.

Death by Death by PowerPoint

And I discovered someone, somewhere, is almost always writing an article called 'Death by PowerPoint'.

It was an easy target when you couldn't think of a subject for your weekly column.

And people with a platform seemed desperately keen to hate on PowerPoint. Writers especially. I remember devouring a book by the excellent technology journalist Clive Thompson and then suddenly being sideswiped by the phrase 'cognitively bleak commercial software packages like PowerPoint…' What!?

My hero, Edward Tufte, was almost always quoted in these Death by PowerPoint articles. He'd decided that it was the very devil and had published a much-cited pamphlet entitled 'The Cognitive Style of PowerPoint', which blamed my beloved piece of software for people's actual deaths. (More on that later.)

I didn't understand why everyone was so contemptuous of a tool I found so joyous and liberating. I understood that bad presentations were bad. I'd sat through a lot of them. But I couldn't quite see why everyone blamed the tool itself. It seemed like blaming pulpits for the boringness of sermons or printing for the tedium of books. I started to get a chip on my shoulder about all this PowerPointHate. This book is me trying to fry that chip with love.

Ministry of PowerPoint

I got a clue about this apparently arbitrary contempt in 2011 when my career took an odd turn and I went to work for a new organisation inside the UK government called the Government Digital Service (GDS).

Our official job was to take thousands of government digital services and websites and make them coherent, consistent and good. Our unofficial job was to help the UK civil service become properly 'digital'. Our plan for doing that mostly consisted of removing power from senior civil servants and large technology companies and giving it to more junior civil servants and people who actually knew how technology worked. We suspected that good communications and great presentations were going to be important weapons in doing that. Officially I was Strategy Director; in practice I was Head of PowerPoint.

Two incidents from that time stick in my mind.

Firstly, very early in the job, I was asked to go and do a presentation about our work at a Very Important Ministry. One of the big ones. Jobs or Money or Foreigners. With Senior Civil Servants.

I arrived with my laptop, was shown into the meeting room, and started to plug it into the projector. It was, of course, an ancient wood-panelled room with a tiny monitor and a massive painting of a nineteenth-century naval encounter.

I was just one part of a day-long series of presentations, so my audience were already seated and waiting while I was plugging in. They chatted among themselves as I did so, discussed fiduciary policy, made jokes in Latin. Then I finished fiddling with the wires and sat politely waiting for the chatting to finish. I waited quite a while. Eventually one of the chatterers broke off from their conversation and came to ask me when the Strategy Director would be arriving. I'm here, I said. He was astonished. Oh, he said, I thought you were the techie.

That was the day I learned that senior civil servants thought that if you understood computers enough to plug a laptop into a projector you couldn't also be capable of doing a presentation to someone of their seniority. That sort of thing happened a lot. Knowing anything about computers was a sign that you were the wrong caste. You weren't equipped to talk to them about policy. It was a bit like the way aristocrats in novels look down on 'trade'.

That disdain extended to file formats. Whitehall culture was based on words, language and argument. They wrote papers and memoranda.

Their meetings were discussions of papers that everyone was supposed to have read but which almost no one had. Those discussions were captured in notes, which were circulated but not read and eventually archived. Useful, difficult decisions were never made because every shade of opinion could simply be added to the paper. Memoranda are infinite. You don't need to decide anything. You can just write it all down. The civil service lived in Word, in .doc.

We, on the other hand, wanted to move quickly and decisively so we decided to work in .ppt. We kept our words very brief and very big. We set very clear presentation rules. Fonts no smaller than 30pt. No more than six words a line. No acronyms. No clip art.

If you don't have many words you have to make sure they're the right ones. Big, brutish and short. We motored through Whitehall processes and procedures by baffling them with clarity. While everyone was still annotating their memoranda we'd made five big, clear points, got everyone nodding along, secured a budget, driven out a corrupt, exploitative technology incumbent and set up an easy-to-use website.

Sort of. Not quite. But sort of.

This was when I realised that the right sort of PowerPoint can be more than a creative sales tool or an intellectual diversion. It can get things done. It can get an organisation to change. Not many things can do that.

The second incident was a tiny historical footnote – the first PowerPoint presentation ever given inside the historic, hallowed and spectacularly ill-equipped Cabinet Room at Number 10 Downing Street.*

After about a year of GDS we'd managed to launch a new government website called GOV.UK and were invited to attend the weekly cabinet meeting to talk about it with the prime minister and, well, the cabinet. This was an enormous deal. Most civil servants, even most senior civil servants, never get to present to cabinet and we were just some interlopers with jeans and laptops. 'Exciting,' we thought, and asked the relevant administrative panjandrums what size screen we'd be presenting on and what cables and connectors we might need to bring. 'Screens?' came back the scoffing reply. 'There are no screens in the Cabinet Room – you'll be expected to present a paper.' Oh, we said, and dug our bureaucratic heels in. We had a pretty strong case. We'd been asked to show the cabinet the new government website; it would have been pretty strange to just read out a paper describing it. After a lot of back and forth we won and arranged to have a screen delivered to Number 10 the evening before the cabinet meeting. A small group of us (the people who would be doing the presentation) arranged to go and meet it and make sure everything worked.

The screen was very late arriving at Number 10, so we spent a long time sitting around in the Cabinet Room, chatting with the Number 10 staff and running through the presentation. We all took turns sitting in the prime minister's chair, chatting, scoffing adequate Number 10 tea and disappointing Number 10 biscuits. I later realised how crucial this was in the presentation going well. Rooms like that are designed to intimidate.

* As far as I know. That's what the Number 10 staff told us.

Imagine having to turn up to a cabinet meeting, wait outside worrying, be summoned in, be stared at by all those important people and have to just start talking. Terrifying.

The next day we were still nervous but we'd already been in the room, we knew the lie of the land. We knew the biscuits were rubbish. That made it a lot easier. The meeting seemed to go well.

(My role in the actual meeting was miniscule. I'd helped write the presentation but my boss did all the presenting. I just sat at the keyboard and pressed the space bar to advance the slides. We knew better than to trust a remote at a time like that. I remember thinking how effective David Cameron seemed to be at running a meeting, and what a rare skill that is. It's not a thing politicians normally put in their campaign material, but maybe it should be.)

Although it seems trivial, I suspect the fact we decided to do PowerPoint at GDS really made a difference. It clarified thinking, it broke through the bureaucratic miasma and it was shareable on social media. It eventually became 'a way' of doing presentations that spread beyond GDS and is seen and used in other organisations. The team I worked with at GDS were frequently asked for advice on how to do those kinds of presentations and after we all left we wrote it up for people at www.doingpresentations.com. It's still there if you'd like to see what we advised.

#notallpowerpoint

One of the Doing Presentations crew was Ella Fitzsimmons.

She taught me the next big thing I learned about PowerPoint.

I was running a training session about presenting. I've done a bunch of these over the years, they normally go OK, but Ella, kindly, firmly and correctly pointed out how useless this training was for anyone who wasn't a tall, white, middle-aged, able-bodied man: i.e. most of the people in the world. She was obviously right. I just hadn't thought about it.

Because I am an idiot (and a tall, white, middle-aged, able-bodied man) my advice about doing presentations had basically been: do it like me, do the things I do – and not everyone can do that.

If you don't have all that privilege you don't automatically get granted attention when you stand on a stage or at a lectern. You can't necessarily do the self-deprecating 'cold open' I often do. You might have to assert some credentials to get people to pay attention. You might have to overturn some stereotypes early on.

You might even be battling against the physical infrastructure of presentations.

The microphones that conference organisers often use, for instance, are designed to clip on to the lapel of a jacket or the placket of a shirt (the bit with the buttons). If you're not wearing traditional masculine dress you might struggle to be mic'd up.

Or you might be given one of those fancy microphones that go over your ear and round your cheek to your mouth. They're great, unless you're wearing earrings. And, for some reason, if you're on a panel or being interviewed on stage you'll often be asked to sit on a high stool and face the audience. Not brilliant if you're wearing a skirt.

Sound systems are tuned for men's voices. Lecterns are terrible for little people. Stages are often inaccessible for wheelchair users (I learned that at Interesting). The list goes on.

Working with Ella made me think about presentation training very differently. And this book would have been very different without her influence; there'd be many more unthinking assertions about how to speak, stand and present yourself. Instead, I've focused my advice on the actual slides and on little tips and tricks that work for me. They might for you. But they might not.

And Ella solidified a thought for me. One that had been bubbling under since Interesting. She even supplied the perfect quote to sum it up: 'Find out who you are and do it on purpose.' Said by the great Dolly Parton.

Another friend and colleague – Rachel Coldicutt – helped me to understand this even better.

We worked together at a digital rights think tank called Doteveryone and were both required to stand on a lot of stages and do a lot of presentations. I was OK at this. People didn't mind my presentations too much.

Rachel is one of the most watchable presenters you'll ever see. If you get the chance, go to one of her talks. This is mostly, overwhelmingly, because she's smart, articulate and funny. She's not just a great speech-maker. She's great at writing interesting slides and interacting with them in dramatic, effective ways.

But at least part of that watchability is also what makes her very nervous about presenting – she has a stammer. Conventionally, this would be regarded as something to 'overcome'. Rachel's written eloquently about it and about her strategies to minimise her blocking. But she's also decided not to let it stop her and to plough on regardless. This is one reason her slides are so great – she has to think carefully about her performance alongside them. Her slides often contain the words that she has trouble saying and she'll just gesture at them. This is a great technique for her, but it'd be brilliant practice for anyone. That kind of interaction with your slides helps a presentation be different and better than a speech.

But, also, Rachel's stammer adds drama and humanity. When Rachel is blocked on a word, the audience can't help but try to guess what it's going to be, which means they're listening hard. It's incredibly compelling. And the stammer also demonstrates how important these words are for Rachel to get out. It's clearly not easy for her to be up there, so, again, you pay attention. You'll remember Rachel's words because they're brilliant. You'll have listened because they're so obviously and uniquely from her.

(I hope this doesn't sound like I think of stammering as an entertainment. That's not what I'm saying. Rachel tells me that she's OK with me finding her stammer very watchable. I hope I don't offend any other stammerers in saying this.)

Bad at PowerPoint

My time at GDS, seeing the disdain that senior civil servants had for PowerPoint, realising that politicians almost never used it and regularly reading the contempt that writers and academics poured on it finally made me wonder whether my reflexive joy in PowerPoint was crazy.

I decided to examine the criticism it was getting. Was there anything to it?

There were some criticisms that seemed fair enough. The clichés you get in any office setting. The jargon, the bad clip art, the stupid graphics. It's easy to make PowerPoint a symbol of bad work and the horrors of organisational life. That's fair enough, I guess. You get the similar jokes about the office coffee machine (though that doesn't lead to polemics in broadsheets about the need to ban coffee).

Then there was the criticism levelled at PowerPoint by people like Edward Tufte. This was about the tool, about the way PowerPoint encouraged you to think and communicate. I didn't agree with this stuff, or at least I didn't think the bad outweighed the good, but I had to accept it was a good-faith, intellectually reputable argument.

Similarly, people began talking about how companies like Amazon had recently 'discovered' the benefits of well-written long-form documents as preparations for decision-making. Again, perfectly valid. Of course, this isn't what PowerPoint is for. But, I couldn't help being annoyed by people reporting this sort of thing as 'Bezos Bans PowerPoint'.

And then there was just plain laziness and snobbery. I'd seen a lot of this in government where we'd run up against senior civil servants, politicians, journalists and academics. Their basic reaction to PowerPoint seemed to be one of distaste. They would sometimes pretend that it was too modern or technical but really they just thought it was beneath them. They didn't understand why people couldn't deliver a speech instead, or just write an elegantly crafted paper or article. They were people of the word; they were suspicious of PowerPoint's ability to incorporate visuals and communicate without language. (And they didn't seem to understand that more junior members of an organisation sometimes don't get the time to craft an elegant paragraph or can't secure the attention to extemporise in front of an all-staff meeting for twenty minutes.)

They were exercising power. PowerPoint is above all a tool that helps you present. It gets you going, gets you from terrified to saying something. It's something to hide behind. It creates access. If you're already in power and you got there by being confident, fluent and good at public speaking then PowerPoint seems simultaneously trivial and threatening.

You see variants of this attitude in business and the military. Every now and then a CEO or general will decide to sweep away PowerPoint and instruct their people to 'just talk about the business'. They forget how easy that is for them to do, and how hard it is for people without power to do the same. PowerPoint levels playing fields, so it's most useful if you're playing uphill.

All of which made me want to write a corrective; something celebratory about PowerPoint, something that pointed out how phenomenally successful it's been. *Wired* magazine were kind enough to commission that and, for the first time, it occurred to me to wonder who'd invented the damn thing in the first place.

Enter Gaskins

Thirty seconds of googling later I was deep in the world of Robert Gaskins and I fell in love with PowerPoint all over again.

The first thing I did was buy and download his book. It's fantastic. It's not just a great book about PowerPoint – it's a great book about creating products and building companies. Detailed, precise, literate. It's indicative of his very dry sense of humour that it's entitled *Sweating Bullets*.

One of the things that quickly becomes apparent is that PowerPoint was actually invented. Creative, structural, novel and non-obvious decisions were made about it. Decisions that were responsible for its success, decisions that summoned a whole software category to life and defined it to this day. Looking back from now, even if you have some awareness that presentations existed before computers, it would be easy to assume that PowerPoint was inevitable – as natural a part of 'office' computing as word processing and spreadsheets.* Not true.

Gaskins made this thing happen.

And he made it a stunning success. It was the first venture capital investment by Apple Computer's strategic investment group. Microsoft and Apple were both serious suitors for PowerPoint because it was one of the few products that made their new world of Personal Computing seem like it might have some practical purpose. That's because Gaskins saw into the future and understood what the PC and a Graphical User Interface might enable. Computers were a big investment back then but businesses would fork out for them just to get PowerPoint. They were buying Gaskin's vision – not Apple's or Microsoft's.

* Both of which were also non-obvious and have their own extraordinary stories.

PowerPoint didn't piggyback on the PC revolution – it helped to create it.

(If my book sparks any interest in you at all, or you're a fan of the TV series *Halt and Catch Fire*, I really would recommend *Sweating Bullets*. I had to fight hard with myself not to just retell the whole story here. Gaskins' insights and anecdotes are much better than mine.)

Reading the book and spending time with Gaskin's superbly curated homepage also made me realise that he's someone who should be more widely known and celebrated. He's the technology hero we should have had.

Not Jobs, Not Bezos

There's quite a lot in this book about Steve Jobs of Apple and Jeff Bezos of Amazon. They're in here because they're relevant, and there are things about PowerPoint to learn from them, but also because they're the kind of rich and famous people who end up in books. And they're rich and famous because they invented things and changed the world by being, among other things, driven, egotistical, disregarding of human feelings, cavalier about legislation and, to use the language of their homeland, jerks. Steve Jobs, for instance, was a great presenter. He also treated people appallingly. The one doesn't make up for the other. But we celebrate him. We write about him. I'm going to do it myself.

Gaskins seems to be cut from a different cloth. He invented something pretty important. And he's pretty proud of it. But he seems to be just as proud of the creation of www.concertina.com (a reference collection of documents for the study of English, Anglo and Duet concertinas), one of his retirement projects. He's a man with interests that don't involve him addressing world leaders or firing things into space. Indeed, his interests beyond technology probably contributed to PowerPoint's success. He studied literature and theatre as well as computer science. He hung an extraordinary collection of contemporary art on the walls of the PowerPoint offices. Edward Tufte is one of PowerPoint's fiercest critics but Gaskins heartily recommends Tufte's books on his homepage. He has enough ego to write a book about his invention, but that book is packed full of acknowledgements that PowerPoint was the product of a team. And the team were non-obvious too. He hired diversely and well. They had unusual backgrounds for a Silicon Valley development team and there were far more women than the average.

You get the picture. I fell slightly in love and am therefore rather intimidated by him. I'm very anxious about what he'll make of this book.

Anyway. I still had to write this *Wired* article and eventually I screwed up the courage to email him. He answered my questions clearly and in detail. What a gent.

Swapping emails with Gaskins, reading *Sweating Bullets* and interviewing people for the *Wired* piece made me realise how many multitudes PowerPoint contained. I wrote thousands more words than I needed for the article. I couldn't stop thinking about it. There's a lot more to this than meets the screen, I thought. I could use PowerPoint to talk about everything I've learned about communications, creativity and people.

If the conceit of this book's title applies anywhere, it's here. Robert Gaskins put humour, imagination and care into PowerPoint. That's what we should put into life. As well as, where possible, concertinas.

2 Power 2 Pointless

Writing the article for *Wired* meant it became even easier for journalists to track me down if they needed a 'voice for the defence'.

That's how I ended up on a BBC Radio 4 programme called PowerPointless. You can detect the agenda from the name.

It was more balanced than the usual 'Death by PowerPoint' piece but it still had a rather removed and distant air to it – *let's examine this thing called PowerPoint. It's not something people like us do, obviously, just those people over there in offices, but, nevertheless, we can examine it as a 'contemporary phenomenon' and have some fun at its expense.*

Looking back, that's when I decided to write this book. PowerPoint should be examined. It's woven itself into our lives, and there are all sorts of interesting things to look at and stories to tell. And, yes, there are stupid uses of PowerPoint.

But it seemed most of the people who'd written about it previously were approaching it as something other people did. It's like they were criticising cars by pointing out that if you didn't know how to drive one you could easily have an accident, and isn't it more natural and normal to just be carried about by servants?

So I'm going to examine PowerPoint as a contemporary phenomenon but I'm not going to treat it as a strange oddity. I'm going to assume you've done some PowerPoint in your time.

Big deck energy

Meanwhile, my career has taken another unexpected lurch and I find myself working for a renewable energy company.

Actual PowerPoint is pretty rare at our place; it's a young, digital business, everything is networked, and most presentations are done with Google Slides, written as collaborative exercises across a team and packed full of emojis. Almost everyone there is twenty years younger than me. They're mostly younger than PowerPoint. They're native to a world of presentation software. I pretend to be an expert in presentations and digital communication but I learn something from my team every day.

And, for the first time in my life, I'm working closely with people who've learned their presentational skills as Management Consultants. Our culture incorporates these disparate styles to great effect – a typical slide features a thoroughly researched, elegantly presented graph about energy usage carefully accented with a massive yellow thumbs-up emoji.

Working there has made me realise that PowerPoint has dialects. Different cultures, organisations and industries create different styles of presentation. It's easy to look from one presentational culture to another and regard the other as 'wrong' but things aren't that simple. Being fluent in those different dialects is a useful life skill.

So that's what we're going to do next. Let's look at some slides!

PART TWO PowerPoint Rules the World

In the beginning was the word

Now there's
PowerPoint

How the hell did that happen?

Imagine being a PowerPoint technician at the UN

Talk about stress.

It's 5 February 2003. The US has been building the case for war with Iraq for several months. Gathering intelligence and allies. Trying to get world opinion on side. US Secretary of State Colin Powell is turning up at the United Nations to persuade the world that there's a solid, evidential case. And he's not just going to make a speech, he's going to use PowerPoint. He's taken something from the private world of briefings and put it on a global stage.

Well, full marks, anonymous technician. You nailed it. The world was plunged into war, but that's not your fault. You got the slides to work.

This is how many of us think of PowerPoint. A tool for institutional persuasion. For effective lying. It's how power makes a point.

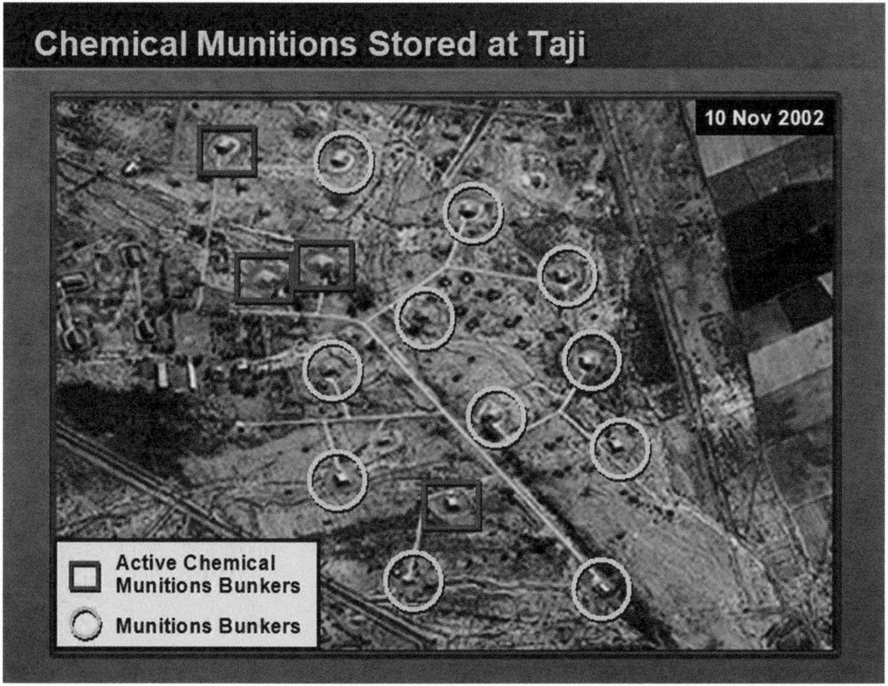

For a while this combination of blue background and yellow type was the way the whole world looked, if you were in a boardroom. PowerPoint nudged you in that direction and few could resist. It fits well with the God's-eye view of the satellite image, reducing all that violent potential to some sort of perverse org chart.

It's the audacious literalism that makes this work. Global culture has spent a decade dancing round the fact that 'the poop emoji' is, literally, a pile of faeces. It's been tamed enough to feature on Christmas cards. But E. B. Tait reclaims and reignites our disgust by labelling it 'shit' and giving it a crown. Our head is shit. And yet we are king. Jaunty angle, too.

But PowerPoint is so much more than that

This is a slide from a presentation by E. B. Tait. She's the daughter of a friend of mine. She's eleven. She uses presentation tools with the casual ease and familiarity with which I once used a space hopper, if I'd been the kind of graceful, physical kid who used a space hopper with ease and familiarity.

She does presentations like this all the time – they're a natural, simple way to communicate, they can incorporate words, images and music, they're easy to put together and share. They have a different quality to a social media post or an email, they're more social, more human. She also enjoys putting swears in them. She was particularly proud of Rick-rolling* her dad with a link one time, which gave her the idea that for her 'what I'd like for my birthday' presentation she could include direct links to the gifts – and that made her wonder whether there's some way to connect directly to the parental bank account and just get the thing paid for from the presentation. I imagine the PowerPoint team are working on that.

PowerPoint is taught in schools, but it doesn't need to be. It's too natural and intuitive. It's as though scrolling on your phone was taught in schools.

* The practise of concealing a link to Rick Astley's 'Never Gonna Give You Up' and tricking someone into watching it. In 2007 it was the funniest thing you'd ever seen. If you're eleven it always will be.

If you want a picture of the future of humanity, imagine a smiley on a Post-it in a PowerPoint deck

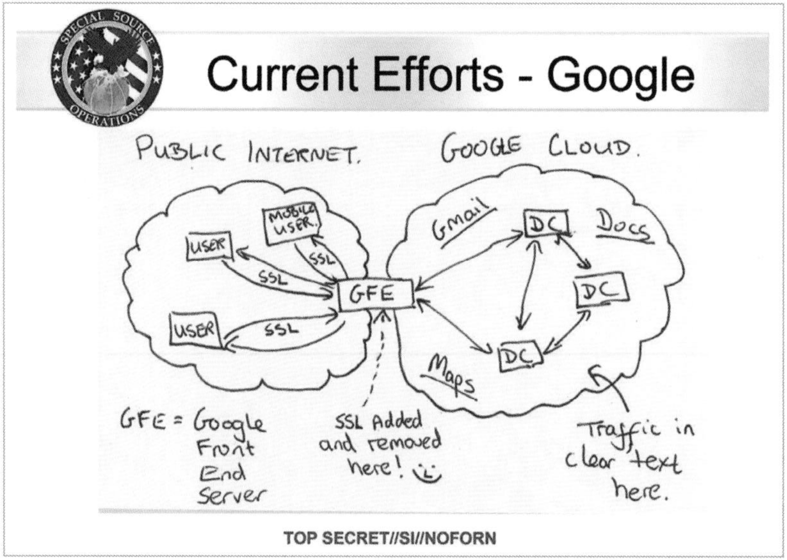

PowerPoint slides are often so distinctive because they are so often pasted into. They're mongrels, happy to accommodate multiple, divergent aesthetics and vibes. Here, for instance, you've got an intricate, grandiose shield from the Military Surveillance Complex, a title bar with a perfunctory nod at a metal effect and a default font choice. All to show us scribbles on a sticky. This is sample culture. This is the aesthetic of COMMAND-V.

This slide is from the huge collection of digital material leaked by Edward Snowden. And this diagram is notorious among internet and security specialists because the phrase 'SSL added and removed here!' reveals an enormous (and previously unsuspected) invasion of big tech company networks by the security services. The stuff in the cloud on the left, which is in 'public', is Google sending data to their users on their phones and computers. This is encrypted so it can't be read by, for instance, the National Security Agency. (That's what the SSL – secure sockets layer – is.) In the cloud on the right is all the stuff happening inside Google's private network, between their own data centres. They'd assumed that didn't need to be encrypted.

But this little cheeky smiley had them panicked. It revealed that the NSA were reading the traffic inside Google's networks. And all the other large computer centres had to assume the same thing too. There was a lot of scrambling to upgrade a lot of stuff.

But there's also something significant about the mode of communication; nerd-scribble on Post-its embedded in a PowerPoint. When I worked in 'digital teams' inside the UK government, we used all the usual modern communication tools – Slack, Trello, Google Slides – and we made quite significant decisions via those tools, decisions about the technical infrastructure of government. Every now and then I'd go and talk in public about that work and the advantages of these tools and I'd bump into historians and journalists who were dismayed by the informal and ephemeral nature of these things. They were still fighting the last war, appalled by the lack of documentation inside Tony Blair's 'sofa' government. They wanted to find 'smoking gun' memos; to pore through archives for written, documented accountability. I had news for those people. This is how these things are decided and recorded now. Little smileys on Post-its. In PowerPoint.

Or maybe it'll save the world

There aren't many presentations that get made into movies

Al Gore's 'An Inconvenient Truth' is one that did.*

Al Gore's interest in environmentalism goes back so far that the first version of this presentation was done with real slides and a real projector. But after he lost the presidential election to George Bush he revived it as a Keynote talk and went on the road, delivering presentations as a route to redemption and meaning. It eventually got made into a movie and helped to provoke interest in the climate crisis. The algore.com website describes it as 'the slideshow that saved the world'.

It also helped popularise a particular form of presentation which has come to dominate the way people do 'talks'; somewhere between a TED talk and Steve Jobs promising to dent the universe with a telephone.

And it showed the world this very specific aesthetic – graphic, clean, minimal words, dark backgrounds – something that sprang from the time it was created, his use of Apple's Keynote software rather than PowerPoint, and the employment of Nancy Duarte. Duarte is probably the most famous and influential presentation designer in the world. Her company has designed more Silicon Valley presentations than any other and she's done more to guide how presentations look than anyone. If you've seen a good-looking presentation it's probably got some Duarte in it.

Of course, not every presentation looks good.

* If you've not seen *An Inconvenient Truth* I can recommend it. The coup de presentation with the cherry-picker is unbeatable.

Another of the gifts PowerPoint has given the world is the normalisation of pixelation. Designers blanche but no one else is really bothered. If you can tell what's going on, why worry? In fact, in this instance, the pixels might be a deliberate aesthetic choice: being badly pixelated makes you look more guilty. This is a magnificent example of the 'kitchen sink' approach to slide design. Every form of emphasis, mixed visual metaphors, some slightly 3D type, lots of CAPS. Let's hope there was also an alarming transition.

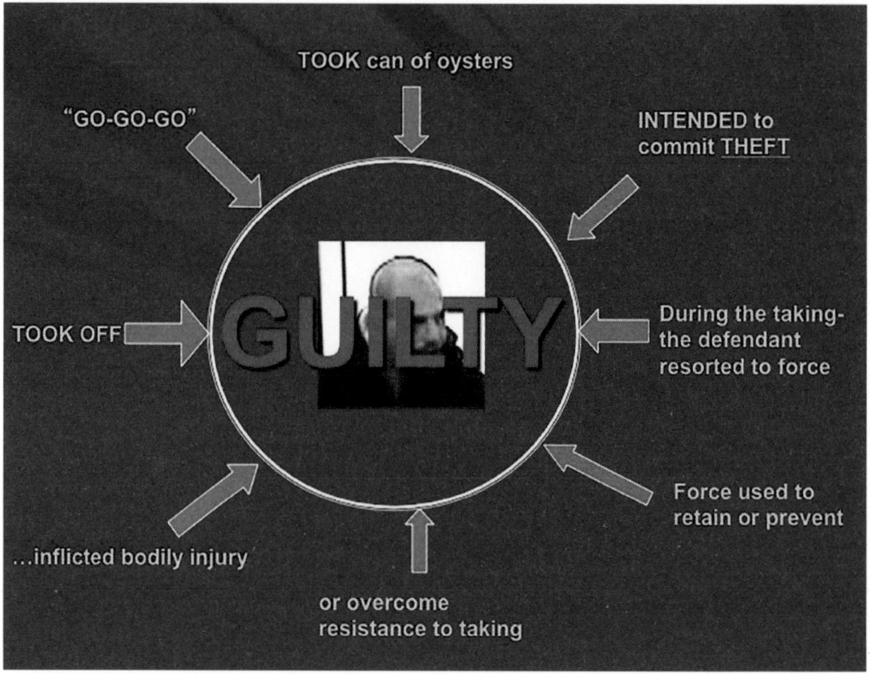

Slide crime

If you ever doubt the power of PowerPoint remember this: it's been legally found, by courts of law, to be unreasonably persuasive. So much so that convictions have been overturned because the prosecutor's use of PowerPoint was deemed to have unreasonably swayed a jury.

In June 2014, for instance, a US court of appeal found that this slide was 'a calculated device employed by the prosecutor to manipulate the jury's reasoned deliberation and impair its fact-finding function'. The court threw out a conviction of life without parole. You can argue as passionately and hyperbolically as you want. But if you start using PowerPoint then a line has been crossed.

It has to be said, prosecutors are not subtle about this stuff. A favourite technique is simply to emblazon the word 'Guilty' across a defendant's photo.

Always in red, blood red.

In 2003 the US National District Attorneys Association (NDAA) published a book that gives tips about using PowerPoint to best effect.
It recommended tricks like this:

Gave a false name to the officer
Unable to explain why in area
I don't know what's in the trunk
Left scene of crime in a hurry
That was not my dope
You can't believe the cops

What jury could resist such compelling logic?

And yet, and yet, the NDAA is probably right. We design snobs can deny it but the point and the power of PowerPoint is that it works even if we don't tidy up the fonts and nicely align the graphics. It's not an exercise in aesthetics, it's about communication.

Ugly slides work. They communicate.

Even Dad Slides.

Dad slides

Politicians haven't embraced PowerPoint. They're one of the very few professions that regularly stands up and talks in front of people without using it. But the coronavirus moment seemed to be one where some decided to try – probably because they were advised that PowerPoint would lend them an air of businesslike competence (while also being a convenient way of displaying charts and graphs).

The most interesting approach to governmental chartage came from the governor of New York, Andrew Cuomo. Partly because he had a strangely compelling way with a presentation, but also because he got subtly picked apart* by media critic and philosopher Shannon Mattern. She published an intricate and fascinating analysis of his presentations which pointed out how he'd managed to merge all sorts of rhetorical devices into his regular pronouncements. How he'd combined the traditional weight and pomp of the New York statehouse with the modernity of two large PowerPoint displays and the formality of his old-fashioned blue suits with an idiosyncratic approach to slide design and language.

It also struck me, watching a presentation Mattern did for the New School, that Cuomo is a pioneer of a genre of PowerPoint I think of as 'Dad Slides'. It is to PowerPoint as Dad Jokes are to humour. This is someone who's not overly worried by traditional aesthetic values. He's happy to chuck in a random chunky arrow, to mix ALL CAPS with sentence case and Bullets With Every Word Capitalised.

Sometimes it feels like traditional PowerPoint. Sensible bullet points about weighty matters. Sometimes he just writes YOU ARE WRONG. That's the subtext for most PowerPoint. Cuomo just wrote it on the slide.

* As I write it's also becoming clear that Cuomo is probably a disgraceful human being.

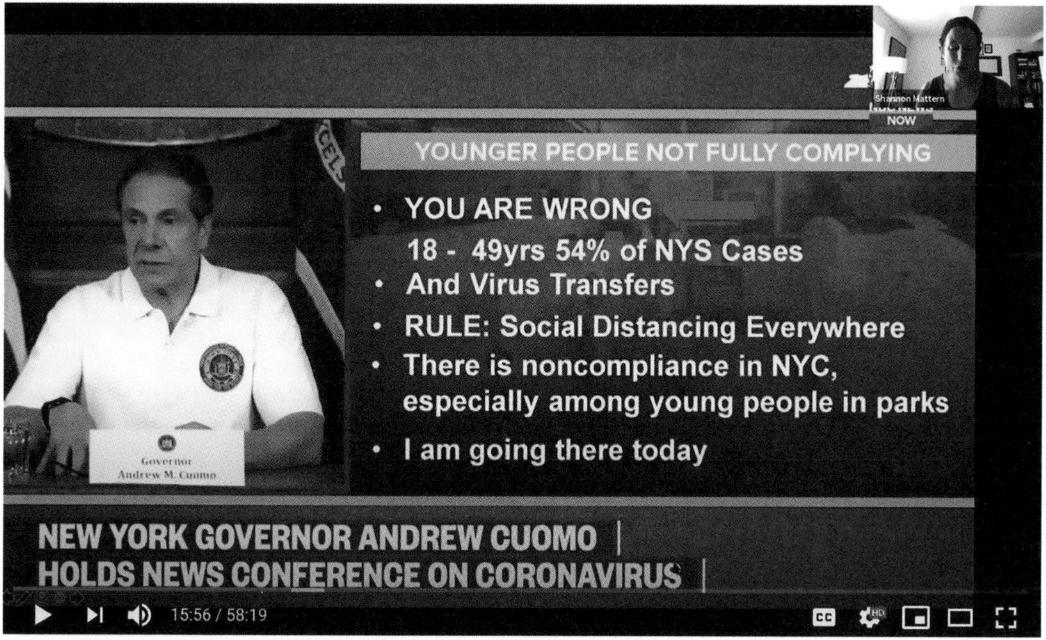

PowerPoint slides are products of PASTE, they are palimpsests, embedding the previous history of the image inside itself. You can see, for instance, that this slide has been transmitted from computer to screen to TV to computer to Zoom to YouTube to book. Or some variant of that journey. And it has survived. Intact. Because it's made of robust communications stuff – big words, a big arrow, not much subtlety. It's not a painting. You don't have to see the brushwork.

This wouldn’t have happened, Theresa, if you’d used PowerPoint

Speeches not presentations

I've always been puzzled by politicians' resistance to PowerPoint.

They stand up and talk a lot. They're mad keen to be photographed in front of stirring but appropriate imagery and concise, powerful phrases. You'd have thought PowerPoint was a gift. And yet, they don't use it; they stand behind lecterns and do speeches. A few good ones can make that work for them; they deliver a memorable soundbite and they get themselves on the evening news but most of them are just dreary and pointless. PowerPoint can't work miracles but it would at least give you something else to look at.

Paul Stephenson and Ameet Gill know more about politicians and communications than most. They've written speeches for prime ministers, won and lost referenda and advised scores of politicians and campaigns. I asked them for theories on this strange aversion.

They came up with these:

1. It's just not in the political culture. Political careers (in the UK at least) are centred on set-piece speeches. Selection meetings. Hustings. Party conferences. The House of Commons. They spend their lives trying to be good at these things – they're not going to waste time learning something else.

2. The trades they tend to come from are also PowerPoint averse – journalism and the law. They just haven't moved in PowerPoint circles.

3. Journalists would take the piss. Any politician caught in charge of a clicker would instantly find themselves on the wrong end of a thousand raised journalistic eyebrows. 'Who do they think they are? A management consultant?' This does not make journalists right. It's just that they're also one of the castes that seldom uses PowerPoint.

Post-pandemic it's going to be interesting to see if they revert to their PowerPoint aversion. I suspect they will.

The PowerPoint and the glory

The PowerPoint dynamics

PowerPoint gets a bad press because journalists don't like it. Neither do cultural critics or academics.

And what do these people have in common?

They're good at writing. Well, they're good at 'writing'. They're good at the sort of long, dense, performatively literate material that got them where they are today. PowerPoint upsets that; it puts communicative power in the hands of people who don't write like that. That's why the media pounces with glee on any story that announces that PowerPoint is bad.

It's as reliable (and untrue) a story as the one that claims that the 18th of January is the saddest day of the year.

And in many organisations the more powerful you get the less PowerPoint you do. Powerful people tend to receive presentations, not give them. And when they do give presentations, they probably won't do their own slides. Someone else will do that for them. Or, very often, they'll stand up and extemporise. Badly. Because no one can stop them.

People in organisations are highly attuned to these signals and behaviours and will therefore assert their own status by distancing themselves from the messy business of PowerPoint production. They'll try to paint it as some sort of lowly, secretarial function, something administrative and tiresome. Men, it seems to me, are especially guilty of this.

Don't do it. Only bad people behave like that.

If you see this happening seize control of the means of PowerPoint. This is your opportunity. This is what the powerful people don't understand. The person writing the PowerPoint is the secret ruler of the org. They have unwittingly put you in charge. You are now monarch of every display.

And what follows power? Art.

Obviously, at some point, the artists show up

I can and will argue that PowerPoint has unleashed more 'folk' creativity than any other single tool. But its ubiquity and power meant that eventually even actual artists noticed it. One of the first and best was *Envisioning Emotional Epistemological Information*, published in 2003, by David Byrne, a book and DVD full of PowerPoint and tiny essays. When confronting PowerPoint most artists make heavy-handed points about mind control or corporate groupthink and Byrne does a bit of this. But he also admits this is an unsurprising response from 'smug pseudo-bohemians like myself' and that there is happiness in surrendering to the affordances and nudges of PowerPoint.

> When you pick up a pencil you know what you're getting – you don't think, 'I wish this could write in a million colors.'

He makes images somewhere between abstract, symbolic and resolutely banal. Like Warhol painting soup tins but with clip art.

Jenny Holzer concentrated on the content PowerPoint produced, the underlying intent, not the manipulative reputation of the tool.

She dug among declassified US government documents and turned briefing slides into large paintings, forcing us to look at what the military industrial complex is presenting to itself.

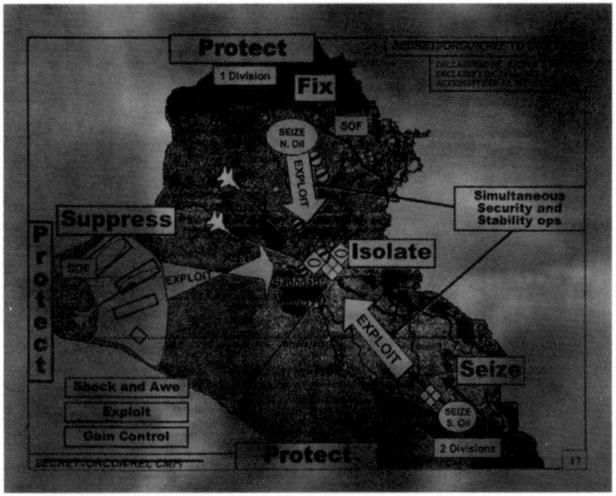

Protect Protect, 2007. Oil on linen, 79 × 102.25 in. / 200.7 x 259.7 cm. Text: U.S. government document. © Jenny Holzer. ARS, NY and DACS, London 2021

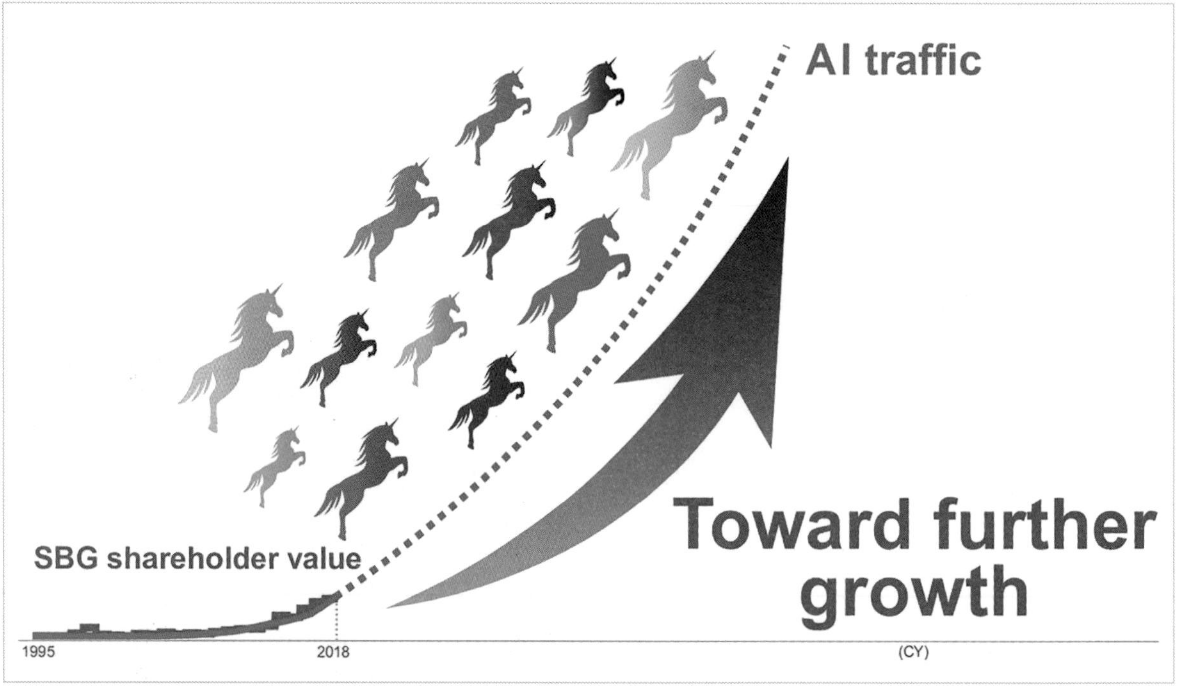

Not all PowerPoint is a bricolage. Some of it has a pure, focused, burning sensibility. I give you, for instance, SoftBank. You could form a religion with the euphoric, polychrome aesthetic of these slides. These are your commandments and your vestments. 'Toward further growth' is all you'd need to say. And then you'd look for the unicorns.

And the artists are left in the dirt

Because, although this looks EXACTLY like a David Byrne image, it is in fact a real slide made by the massive, slightly lunatic Japanese business combine SoftBank to explain how it was going to ride a series of AI unicorns into the future.

Apologies. I should unpick that a bit, shouldn't I.

AI = Artificial Intelligence.

Unicorns = business slang for private companies valued at more than a $1 billion (many of which are invested in by SoftBank).

The future = where SoftBank founder Masayoshi Son is going to live and where you and I, probably, are not. Masayoshi Son's presentations have become legendary in the business/investment/snarky internet world. His presentations are as exuberant as E. B. Tait's and he is unafraid to thoroughly explore a metaphor via clip art.

For instance, when explaining to sceptical investors how SoftBank would cope with the effects of the pandemic, the global recession and his own spectacularly misjudged investment in WeWork, he decided the best bet was an extended analogy about ponies falling into a 'valley of coronavirus' from which some emerge by turning into unicorns and flying out.

You and I might want to laugh at this. Bully for us. But we're not managing billions of dollars of investments, and as the *FT* commented:

> Jokes aside, in a way it feels sort of right to us. The deck is basically saying one-third of us will happily exit this economic trough on the same trajectory we did before: think of those who work in essential services, or run a video streaming platform, or offer an online-shopping experience ... While the remaining 66 per cent – the travel companies, restaurants and advertising-spend dependent among us – will remain firmly stuck in the economic mire ... It seems as valid a thesis as any.

(We will ignore the fact that, classically, unicorns don't fly, because this slide is batshit genius.)

Think till our brains crush

We all know what corporate values are normally like. This sort of thing:

> **RESPECT**
> **INTEGRITY**
> **COMMUNICATION**
> **EXCELLENCE**

Most of us work somewhere with values like these. They are generally bland, hard to remember and ineffective. These are, for instance, the corporate values of Enron. Which demonstrates just how effective corporate vision statements are in preventing your company's collapse into corruption and criminality.

Not SoftBank's though. SoftBank's values are an overwhelming No. 1.

This is what I love about PowerPoint.
It encourages speech, it fosters creativity, it's a way for oddness and eccentricity to spill out into cultures that normally try to eradicate anything unpredictable and off-piste.

Press releases aren't allowed to be like this. Annual reports don't normally contain sustained similes involving ponies, valleys and unicorns. (Though SoftBank's might.) These things are typically scrubbed clean of anything aberrant and unexpected. But presentations get a pass, presentations are allowed to be different. Because they are different. Because PowerPoint.

(We have to grant SoftBank the possibility that some of the clarity was lost in translation. We can see what 'Think till our brains crush' might originally have been trying to say. But 'No revolutions are down to the earth' is harder to parse. Is that an environmental message, advocacy for more space-based programmes or an injunction to forget workaday realism? Does it matter? No.)

SoftBank Values

1) Focus on information revolution and contribute to people's happiness

2) Be ambitious and tenacious of justice

3) Commit to be an overwhelming No.1

4) Think till our brains crush

5) No revolutions are down to the earth

⋮

There's something here that reminds me of a modernist church. The design is clean and sharp. Almost brutal. The decorative elements seem like discarded punctuation. But the language is a religious mix of the gentle and the extreme. You could imagine this carved in marble or concrete.

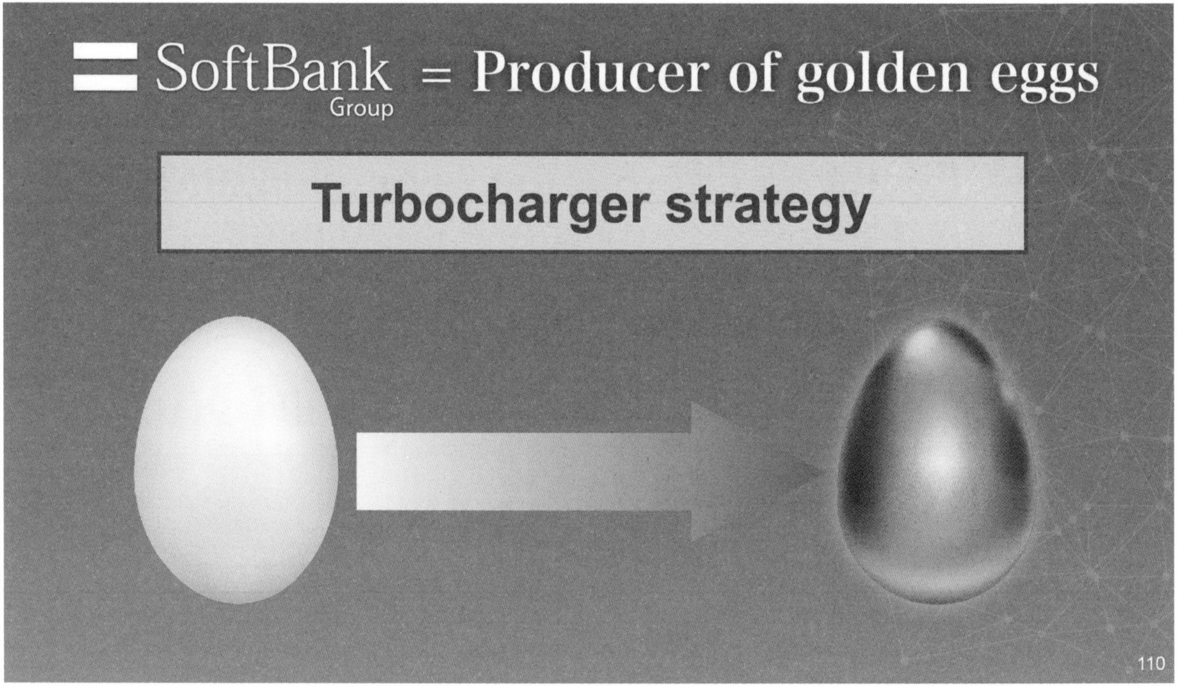

There is a mind at work here. An artist. This is not random, last-minute copying and pasting. This is world-building. The deliberate evocation of an alternate reality. Here, for instance, the gold, the sky-blue background and the simplicity of the narrative implied by the arrow deliberately recalls the best sort of illustrated fairy stories.

Look. Just one more. They're geniuses. Imagine being presented with that. What could you say?

I love the mixing of metaphors. That's not what a turbocharger does. That's not what a golden egg is about. And yet, it's a brilliantly striking image.

There's a term used in aesthetics: *Gesamtkunstwerk*. It's a German loan word that literally means 'total artwork'. It originated with Wagnerian opera; it's an all-encompassing sweeping up of every conceivable art form into a single experience. That's what a SoftBank presentation is. *Gesamtkunstwerk*.

OK. While we're doing crazy, let's talk about the military and why presentations are better than books.

CENSORED

'When we understand that slide, we'll have won the war'

General Stanley McChrystal, the commander of NATO and US forces in Afghanistan, apparently said this when confronted with a particular PowerPoint slide during a briefing.

This is referenced a lot by people who want to tell you how bad PowerPoint is. (And sometimes relatedly, how bad US military strategy is.) People cite it as evidence that the US military had been taken over by 'PowerPoint rangers' and that they are bogged down in bureaucracy and confusion – exemplified by an overcomplicated bit of presentation software.*

I'm not sure it's all that simple. Yes, it's a complex graphic. But that's what Afghanistan was like.

* If you'd like to see this slide just Google the phrase 'when we understand that slide, we'll have won the war'. It's all over the internet. But when I tried to reproduce it for my *Wired* article we received an immediate email asking us to remove it. Maybe it's not quite censorship, but while I'd happily show you that slide in a presentation, my publishers were reluctant to put it in a book.

It's an intensely detailed and intricate map of the relationships and power structures of the country. McChrystal was right. If the American forces could have internalised and dealt with all that complexity they'd have gone a long way to resolving the conflict.

Maybe the anonymous PowerPoint artist was on to something. After all, this particular slide is strikingly similar to Jeremy Deller's famous artwork *The History of the World*, which has been widely praised for revealing the previously hidden connections between acid house, brass bands and the miners' strike. If Deller can 'solve' British culture with a mind map maybe the US military can do the same for Afghanistan.

Maybe not. But more importantly, it's crucial to the understanding of McChrystal's slide to see it in the context of the normal output of the Military PowerPoint Complex, which makes this kind of thing look utterly banal.

Military PowerPoint is all like

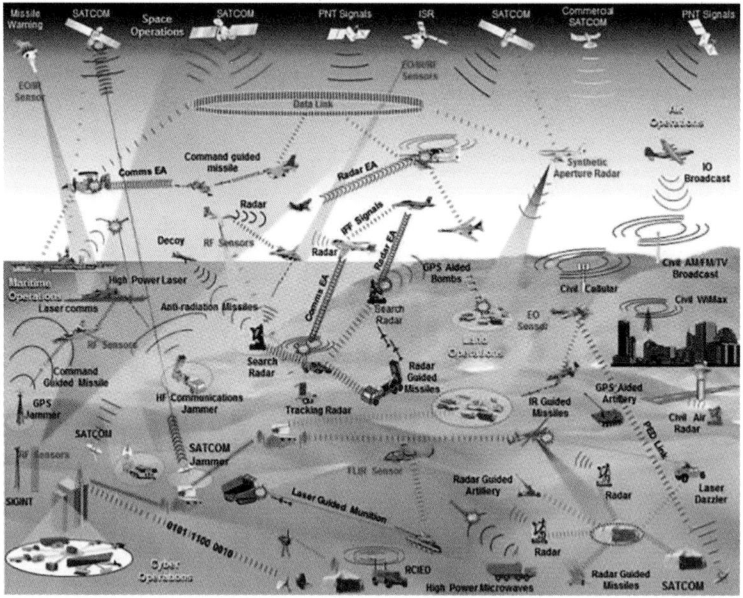

What's striking here is the contrast between the presumed intent of the artist and the actual effect on the viewer. I think we can assume that the brief for this slide was 'illustrate overwhelming and comprehensive capability'. The actual impression delivered is 'we're just making stuff up'. It's the flat background that does it, like a child's play mat. And the sense that the artist has opened a library of military clip art and done SELECT ALL.

The Military PowerPoint Complex

Technologist and writer Paul Ford has developed an obsession with the US military's use of graphics. He's tracked down thousands of US military documents sitting on public servers in PDFs and PowerPoint decks. As he points out on his blog, the graphic language of these things is both extraordinary and everyday:

> Part of what makes military diagrams so fascinating is that they look a lot like the images civilians use to do their regular workaday jobs. It's just software and hardware, after all, and there are only so many ways to draw a network diagram. Yet the scale of these systems is immense; the lines being drawn are between jets and satellites, not between a couple of web servers. You can smell the money burning. Also there is a foundational fact that applies to each image: no matter how abstract they are, these pictures describe systems that the US military uses to make optimal, efficient decisions about killing other humans.

This is PowerPoint at its purest: extraordinary creative freedom mixed with minimal aesthetic training. It lets the unconscious pour out and show what organisations are really like. In this instance it's the banality of clip art presenting the venality of war. In many large organisations it reveals just how utterly incredible it is that they're still going.

You can see evidence for this all over the internet. Just google the phrase 'sony powerpoint leak' and you'll find a 2014 *Gawker* article with the headline 'Sony's Embarrassing Powerpoints Are Even Worse Than Their Shitty Movies'. It's not wrong.

(Paul Ford's blog is at https://ftrain.medium.com/, and most of these slides are courtesy of the joyous Twitter account @defensecharts.)

One's first thought here is 'this is not how onions work'. It seems to be trying to convey concentric circles, layers of survivability, and so you think again and realise that, yes, onions have layers. They are the cliché image for that. So why does this confuse? Maybe it's the wrong cross-section. Maybe it's the overlay of actual concentric circles. Maybe it's the inclusion of the stalky bit at the top. Maybe it fails because the onion is too literal. We will probably never know. Still, 'Don't Be Killed' is always useful advice.

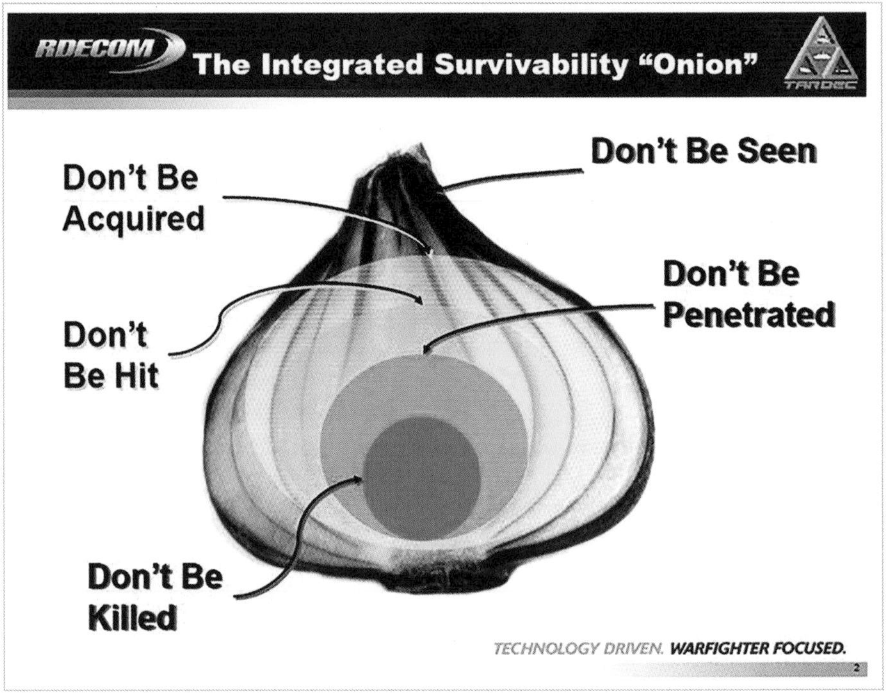

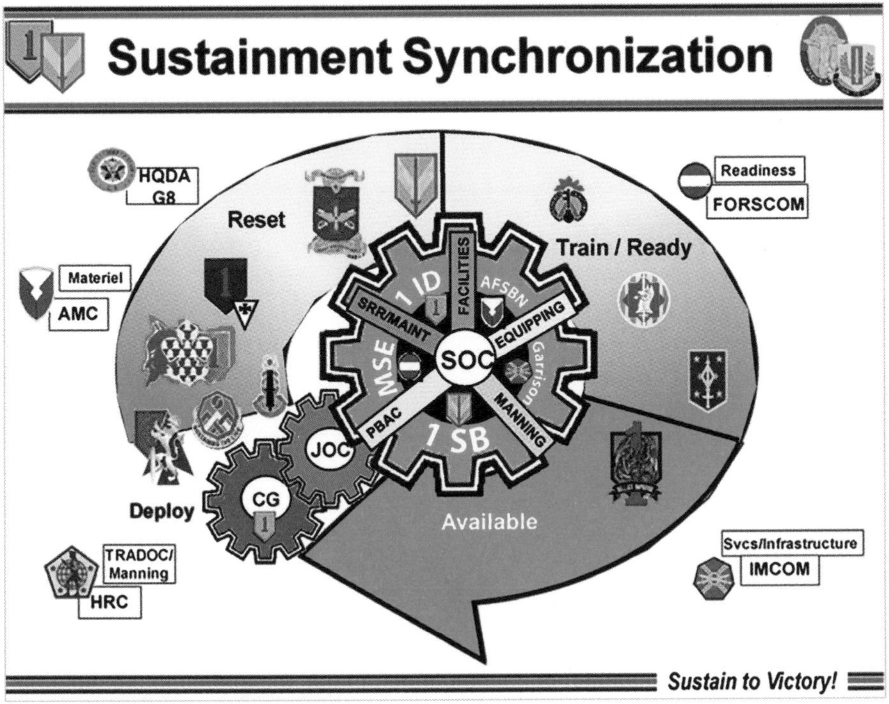

The sheer visual exuberance on display here is topped off by world-class use of jargon. What is 'sustainment'? And is this really how you should ensure its synchronisation? Big swoopy, circling arrows like this are as characteristic of fin-de-siècle PowerPoint as people with one eye are of Bayeux tapestries. They're normally deployed to indicate some sort of repetitive, cyclic process but in this instance the arrow points to absence. Our sustainment is 'available' but then gone. Such is life.

The most common corporate PowerPoint error is simple: too much stuff on one slide. No one is better at this than the military. When faced with a problem people instinctively try to solve it by adding things, rather than taking things away. These slides are an aesthetic manifestation of that phenomenon. You can imagine the conversation: 'I'm not quite sure what this slide is telling me, Corporal.' 'No problem, ma'am, I'll just add some more lines connecting everything to everything else.' This is, of course, the Buddhist response, because it demonstrates the interconnectedness of all things. And we should be fair. Not all these slides are from the US. One represents the UK army. See if you can work out which…

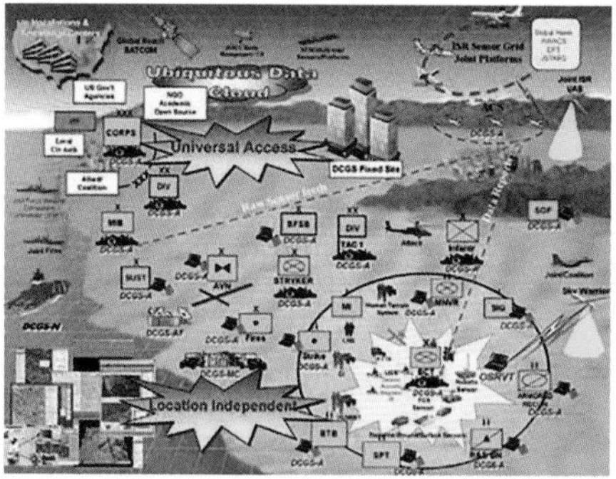

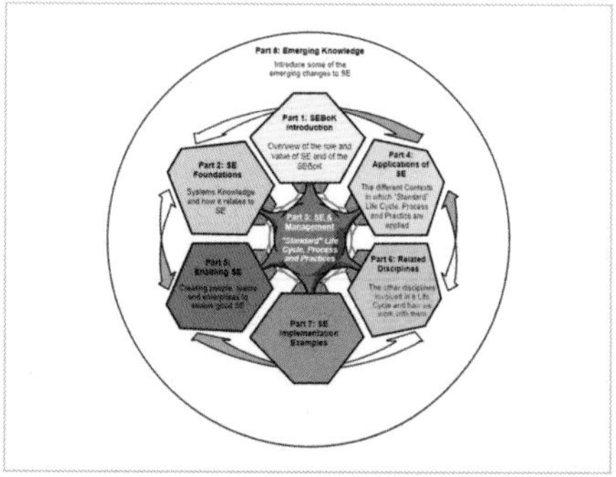

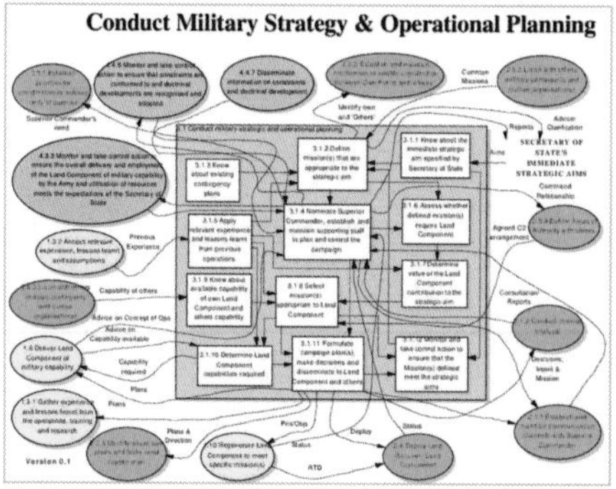

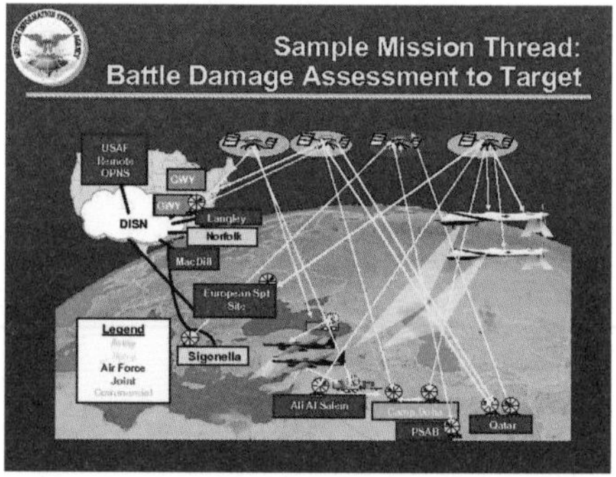

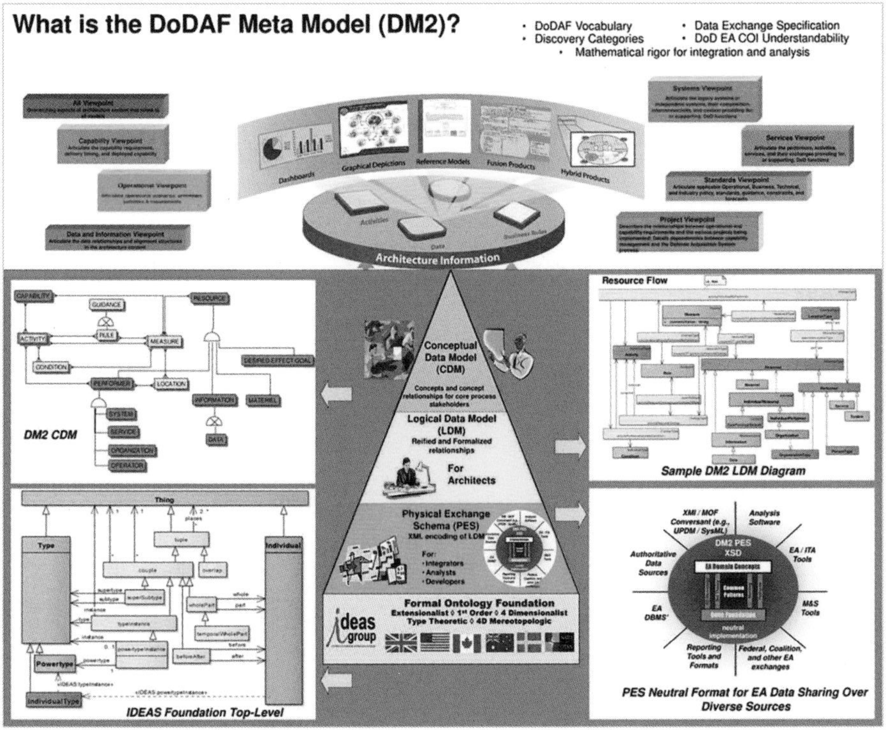

What is the DoDAF Meta Model (DM2)? This slide doesn't offer to explain, it defies you to find out, offering you clues in the form of indecipherable text and impenetrable sigils. It's the PowerPoint equivalent of a medieval labyrinth, designed at first to baffle and confuse, with excursions into strange symbology and signs of mysterious connection. Enlightenment will only arrive after long periods of study and reflection. Dare the artist make the type smaller? Oh yes, they dare. This text is not to be read but to be felt.

Later in this book I will advise you not to worry too much about graphic design. People spend too long being anxious about it when they should just be practising their slides. BUT there is a minimum standard. If you're doing a slide that includes the phrase 'resistance to nuclear use', which presumably indicates quite an important presentation, please try to be professional enough to draw a proper arrow. Wobbly lines don't reassure. Just as there is 'display value' in obviously labour-intensive PowerPoint, perhaps apparent incompetence is really a subtle strategic feint. Sun Tzu said that 'all warfare is based on deception'. Perhaps a twenty-first-century Clausewitz would add that 'war is a continuation of PowerPoint by other means'.

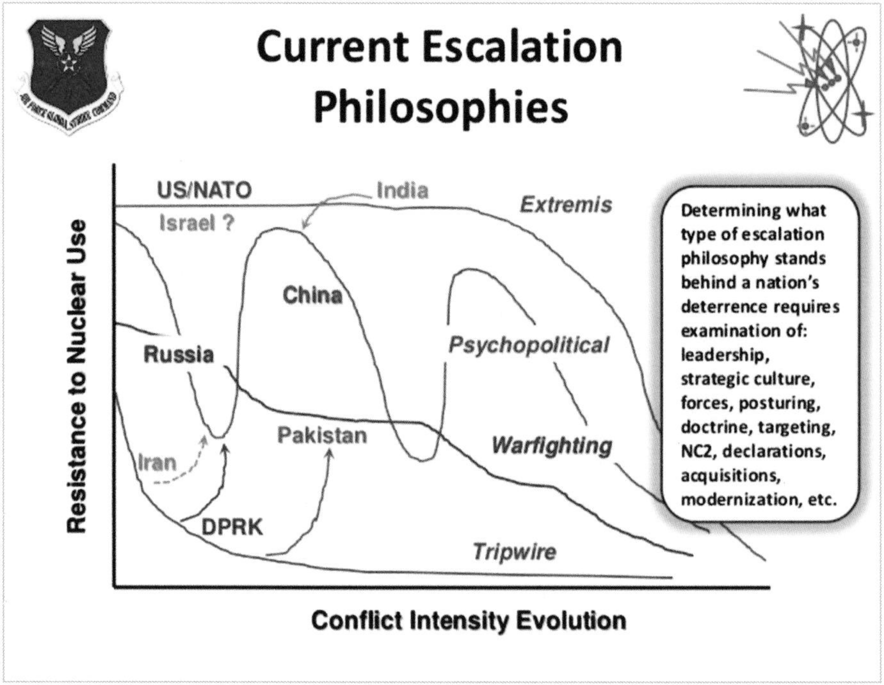

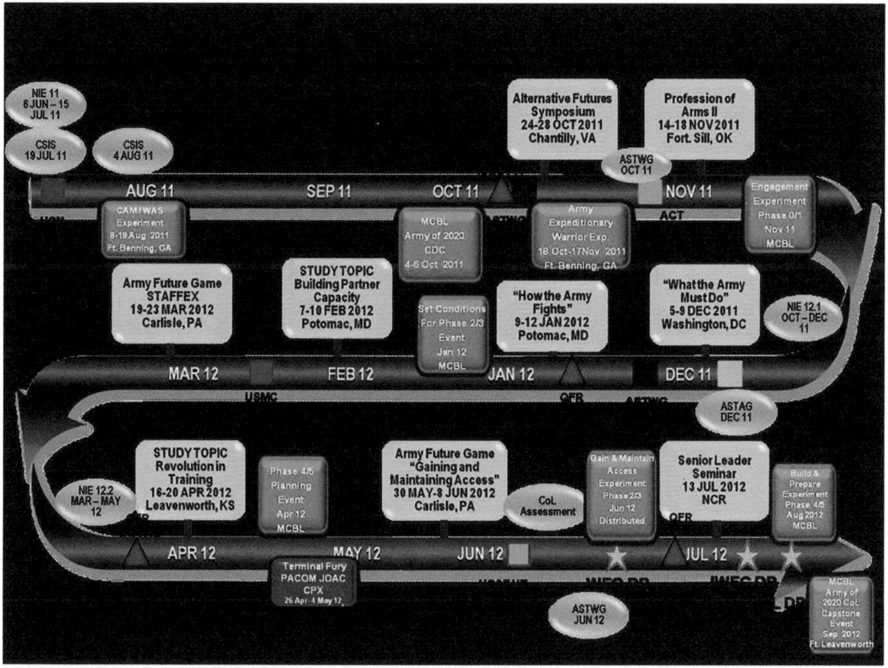

And then you just have to stand up and applaud the PowerPoint technician who decided they wanted to use their afternoon reproducing Donkey Kong. It also might occur to you to wonder whether the evident craft and painstaking care that went into this slide has a similar function to the laborious attention to detail manifest in a Louis Vuitton handbag; the display of wealth and power. Look, this slide says, my unit has such abundant resources that we can afford to spend time and energy creating a slide with no obvious communicative value. It is a peacock's tail. A display of wasteful masculine virility.

4
4
2

If you want to understand an organisation, ask to see the PowerPoint

Three stories:

Sam Allardyce, England football manager for a brief bit of 2016, wrote in his autobiography that his chances of being manager earlier, back in 2006, were damaged by the Football Association's lack of PowerPoint:

> I wanted to do a real knock-your-socks-off interview for the FA, so I put together a PowerPoint which looked at every single detail. There was nothing missing. Nobody but nobody was going to beat it. But then Brian Barwick, the chief executive, told me there were no PowerPoint facilities at the interview venue, so I had to print off hard copies for the panel.

They hired Steve McClaren instead. England failed to qualify for Euro 2008.

Employees of a certain large, Scandinavian, not-as-successful-since-the-iPhone-came-along phone company were so addicted to PowerPoint that if they wanted to meet for lunch they'd open a PowerPoint slide, type 'fancy lunch?' and email it to their colleagues.

A certain large Japanese car company was bound by a corporate regulation that said no presentation could last longer than three slides. Lots of companies have similar rules. Employees, unable to share their work satisfactorily, would cram more and more material on to each slide. You'd end up with screeds of thick, dense text, as small as 6pt (about this size), packed into squares and shapes around the slide. With multiple graphs and diagrams on each slide.

Then each slide would be beamed at the meeting and presented for half an hour. Three slides. Two hours. No one able to read anything. I've been in those meetings.

With these bullet points I thee wed

- ✔ Love
- ✔ Cherish
- ✔ Honour
- ✘ Obey

By the PowerPoint vested in me

I said I wouldn't do that. It's easy to take the mickey out of some bad PowerPoint leaked on to the internet. I'd be equally embarrassed about many of my old slides.

So that's enough.

Let's remember that we get this extraordinary material because PowerPoint is an explicitly creative tool that millions and millions of people are extremely comfortable using. And because it doesn't have many of the gatekeepers and taste-police of other media types.

It gets everywhere and it gets used for everything. Which is why you now get wedding PowerPoint. It's why you now get best man speeches done as PowerPoint, eulogies done as PowerPoint, everything done as PowerPoint, and the weird, joyous exuberance of this stuff is magnificent. Get yourself on TikTok and chase down the lockdown sensation #powerpointparty. You'll find families and groups of friends holding mini-conference events where they all get up and do a PowerPoint presentation.

The topics addressed make you wish that all these talks had been streamed. A random selection:

Why Either One of the Cuomo Brothers Are Anything You'd Want in a Man

Why I Should be Tazzed Awake Every Morning

Femboy Hooters: Would it Work?

Why Pretzels Are Just Confused Bagels

Elephants

Casting Ratatouille – Live Action

Stuff on Graham's Computer

When They Lost Your Luggage and You Need to Buy Underwear: A Geography Lesson

Why Dora Is the Worse Explora

Which War Crimes the Characters of Glee Would Commit

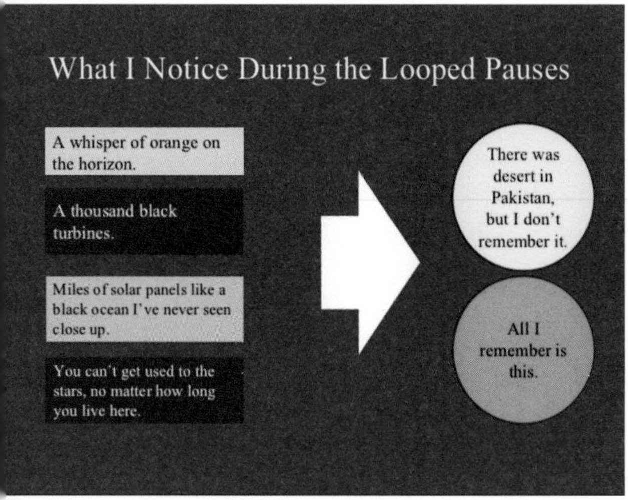

And eventually even the writers will notice

Jennifer Egan's 2010 book *A Visit from the Goon Squad* contains a chapter in PowerPoint, as written by her character Alison. It's not like normal human PowerPoint, but it's illuminating for that reason. Egan talked about it in an interview with the Bookbrowse website:

> I'd also become obsessed with the idea of writing a story in PowerPoint – a program I did not own and had never used. I remember exactly when that idea came to me: I was reading an article about the Obama campaign's turnaround two summers ago, and it mentioned that a particular PowerPoint presentation about the campaign's shortcomings had led to a successful strategy shift. The fact that the presentation in question wasn't referred to as a 'paper,' or a 'document' or a 'memo,' but as a 'PowerPoint,' really struck me. I thought: PowerPoint has become a literary genre; I'd love to write a story in it.

Perhaps because she approaches it naively and as a literary tool she sees through it to something essential. PowerPoint is about moments and pauses. That makes it an unusual media format:

> *Goon Squad* is a book about time, composed of thirteen discrete stories separated by gaps. And PowerPoint (or any slideshow, it doesn't have to be Microsoft) is a genre composed of discrete moments separated by gaps. As a genre, it echoes the structure I was already working with in *Goon Squad*, and its corporate coldness allowed me to be overtly sentimental in ways I probably wouldn't have allowed myself to in conventional fiction.

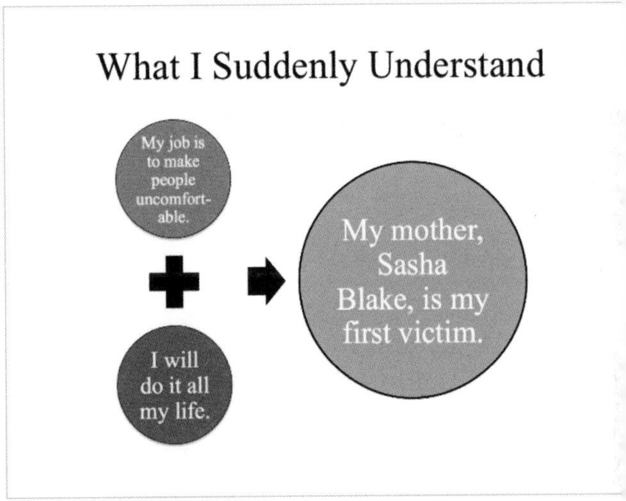
What I Suddenly Understand
My job is to make people uncomfort-able.
I will do it all my life.
My mother, Sasha Blake, is my first victim.

Egan's response to PowerPoint is more writerly than Byrne's. She's barely even making design choices here, using default fonts and shapes, probably a pre-selected palate. But, the simplicity has a stark and effective beauty. She creates a digital *objet trouvé*, a meditation on the technological sublime embedded in the technologically mundane. She uses PowerPoint poetically, to frame words in space and hence in time, to make us see 'pauses' in front of us and to feel them in the transition between slides.

Y tho?

How has PowerPoint become so ubiquitous and powerful?

What is it about this odd bit of software?

A cash point
gives you cash

PowerPoint
gives you power

If MORE ruled the world

People look at PowerPoint now and think its concept and design were obvious. They'll point back at the overheads and 35 mm slides used by previous generations of presenters and think just sticking them on a digital screen was a slam-dunk idea. It was not.

There's a plausible alternative universe where this is a book about MORE.

MORE was an outliner. It worked like this:

You type the headlines, you type the supporting points, you move them around until your argument is complete.

You are done.

This is a perfectly respectable way of doing things. It's very logical, very rational, very Silicon Valley. It's what your typical software engineer might do. And when Gaskins was trying to persuade computer companies of the merits of PowerPoint (called Presenter at the time), a chap called Dave Winer was also talking to them about an outliner program called MORE. It was sophisticated and simple – it let you construct an argument, an outline, and then, if you wanted to present it, print it out as slides. It would automatically arrange everything on the page for you. You'd make no decisions about the way it looked. Winer, quoted here in *Sweating Bullets*, saw this as an enormous benefit of the outliner approach:

> I've always felt that graphics products like page-layout programs, draw programs, paint programs, were too low-level to be useful to word-and-concept people. With MORE, the process of producing graphics was automated. The user didn't get control over every pixel in the presentation, that's the usual tradeoff, but you could produce a sequence of bullet charts in MORE simply by typing in an outline and flipping a switch. It was this instant graphics, its very high leverage, that made MORE a powerful product … I look back on MORE as the perfect product.

This was by no means a minority view. It still isn't. For many people the outline is the presentation. The words are the point and everything else is flim-flam. You'll see an outliner baked into almost every presentation tool, including PowerPoint.

But Gaskins was convinced that the outline-centric model for presentation software was wrong:

> There were always 'outlining people' who thought this way – that a hierarchical outline was the natural structure for representing anything, and that the advantages of being able to achieve precise graphical control were less important than the disadvantage of having to bother with that precise graphical control. The challenge in designing PowerPoint was to reverse that balance in favor of direct visual control by the user ... The structure of a presentation is not the tree of a multi-level outline, but is a single ordered sequence of slides, with each slide having a separate internal structure.

Making PowerPoint slide-centric was Gaskins' first great decision.

There's a magnificent book by Claire L. Evans called *Broad Band: The Untold Story of the Women Who Made the Internet*. PowerPoint doesn't figure in it much – until recently it's not been a very internet-y bit of software – but there's a fascinating chapter on hypertext that explains quite a lot of why we find PowerPoint useful to think with.

We now think of hypertext as being the way the web works: you click on something, it takes you somewhere else. It's a way of linking documents. But the idea of hypertext preceded the web and so did lots of smart thinking about how documents and programs can help us access and understand information. Although they didn't intend this and will probably mock me for suggesting it, I think a lot of this community's thinking about hypertext explains why PowerPoint is so powerful.

Look at PowerPoint in Slide Sorter view and you get presented with a grid of little cards. Like notecards on a pin board. You can move them around to organise your story.

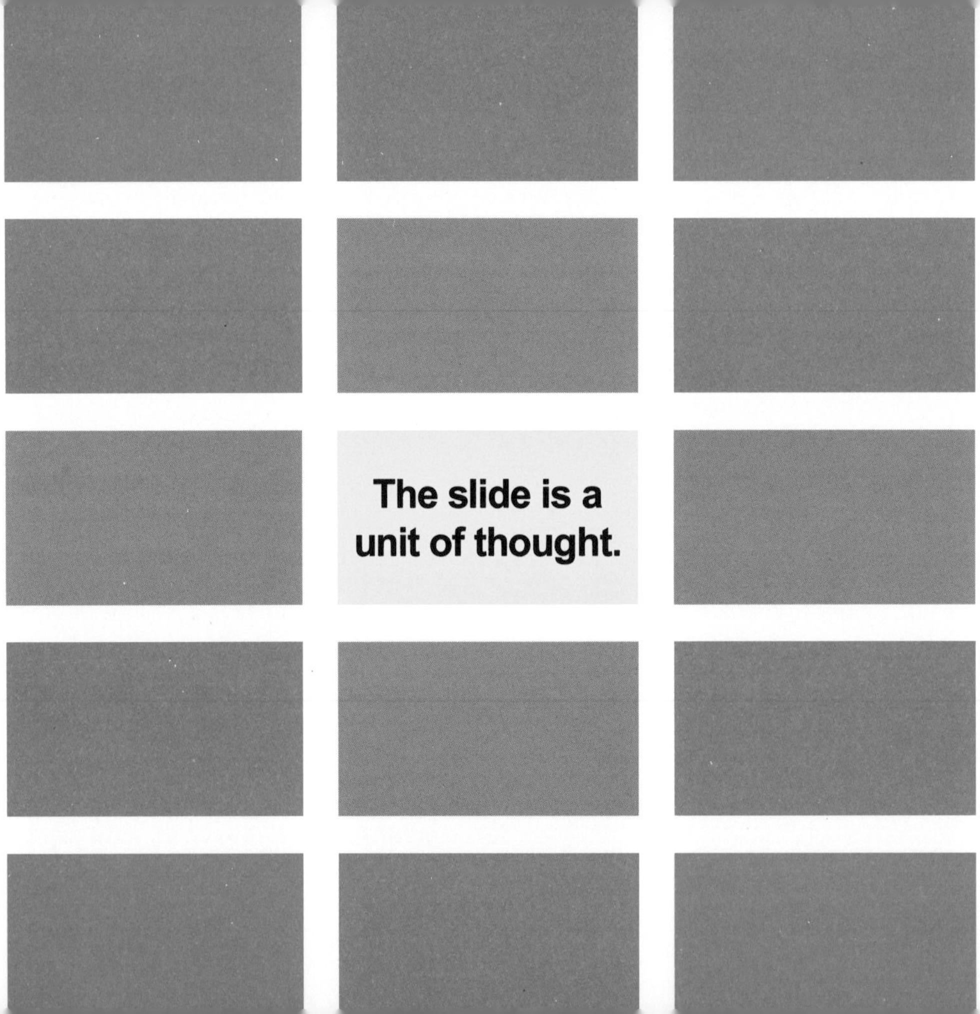
The slide is a unit of thought.

Hypertext thinking – manifest in products like HyperCard – holds that this is a natural way for people to manage knowledge and that getting it on to a screen is a useful way to interact with information. This seems obvious to us now. It wasn't always so. Evans interviews Cathy Marshall, a researcher at the famous think tank Xerox PARC, who investigates what she calls 'knowledge structuring':

> Her hypertext systems were meant to empower kinesthetic thinking, the process of moving things around and trying them out akin to 'wiggling molecular models in space or moving a jigsaw puzzle piece into different orientations'.

PowerPoint encourages this kind of kinaesthetic thinking. Firstly because a slide is a unit of thought we can manipulate. Secondly because adding words and images together makes them more memorable and that means they stick in our head, incorporating us into the system. That, according to Cathy Marshall, is what makes these systems work.

> ...the only important thing is what stays in your head. If my documents, strewn on my desk or clustered as icons on a screen, appear inscrutable to an outside observer, that's no flaw in my system. They should be meaningless, because they're only the remnants of a transformation process, like a sheaf of molted skin. The real technology is the user.

Blessed be the content originators

Gaskins' second great idea was to let people muck about

Just as there have always been people who don't value the graphics much, there have always been those that say users shouldn't be allowed to make ugly slides. It would be perfectly possible, they maintain, to constrain the choices available so as to make unfortunate colour combinations or tiny fonts impossible to select. Imposing taste and subtlety on people and causing eternal happiness for all.

Gaskins rejected this idea. He wanted the people giving and creating presentations to have as much control as possible. He knew these people existed; he knew there would be more of them. There wasn't a word for them, so he called them 'content originators'. They wanted to communicate ideas; he wanted them to love PowerPoint:

You can see this motive called out in the very first description of PowerPoint that I ever wrote, almost three years before PowerPoint 1.0 shipped. In the list of proposed 'user benefits', the culminating line is 'Allows the content originator to control the presentation' (this line is even italicised – the only italics in these two pages). The term 'content originator' was the best I could devise to mean 'business people responsible for thinking up ideas and gaining assent to them'. A word like 'executive' or 'knowledge worker' sounded too much like a bureaucrat, and that didn't capture my idea of the people who would most intensely love PowerPoint. A bureaucrat churning out boilerplate doesn't care that much about the details of quality, but a thinker trying to gain assent to an original idea cares passionately about giving it the best shot possible, because the result makes a real difference to the presenter's personal and business success.

Not your typical software team

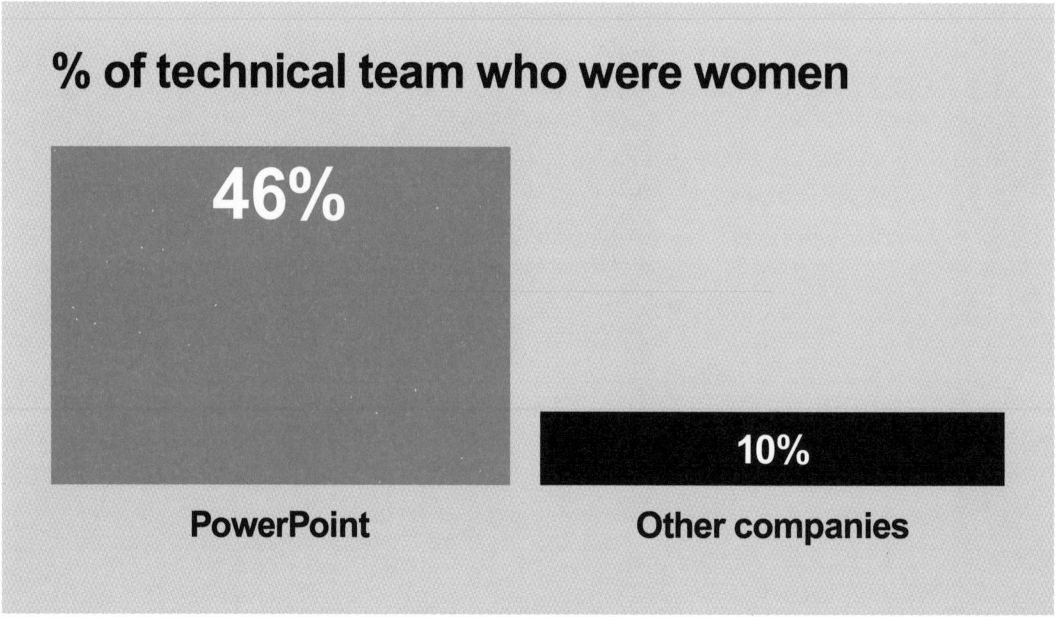

He was able to make these decisions and build such a user-centric product because he wasn't a typical software engineer and he gathered non-typical people around him.

Here's Robert:

> While never compromising on computer science knowledge and ability, I consciously tried to find people who also had broader interests in other fields, including social skills and communication skills. We hired developers with undergraduate and graduate degrees in liberal arts or science disciplines as well as computer science, and with experience of many different kinds, both academic and commercial.
>
> The people we were looking for were unusual – then and now. To find them, we tried to attract the smartest people, with a variety of backgrounds and with broader education and skills than most software start-ups. The resulting difference in our people should be a big part of the reason for PowerPoint's success.

A huge body of evidence is emerging that proves that the best way to improve the performance of a team is to increase the number of women in it. Maybe that too is part of the explanation for PowerPoint's success.

> Out of sixty contributors who joined us while I headed the group, more than half (53 per cent) were female; among all our people in technical jobs, 46 per cent were female, and 60 per cent of all females were in technical positions. When I left Microsoft in 1992, half (3 of 6) of senior department managers reporting directly to me were female.

At the time the average proportion of women in Silicon Valley technical positions was about 10 per cent. Today it's around 20 per cent.

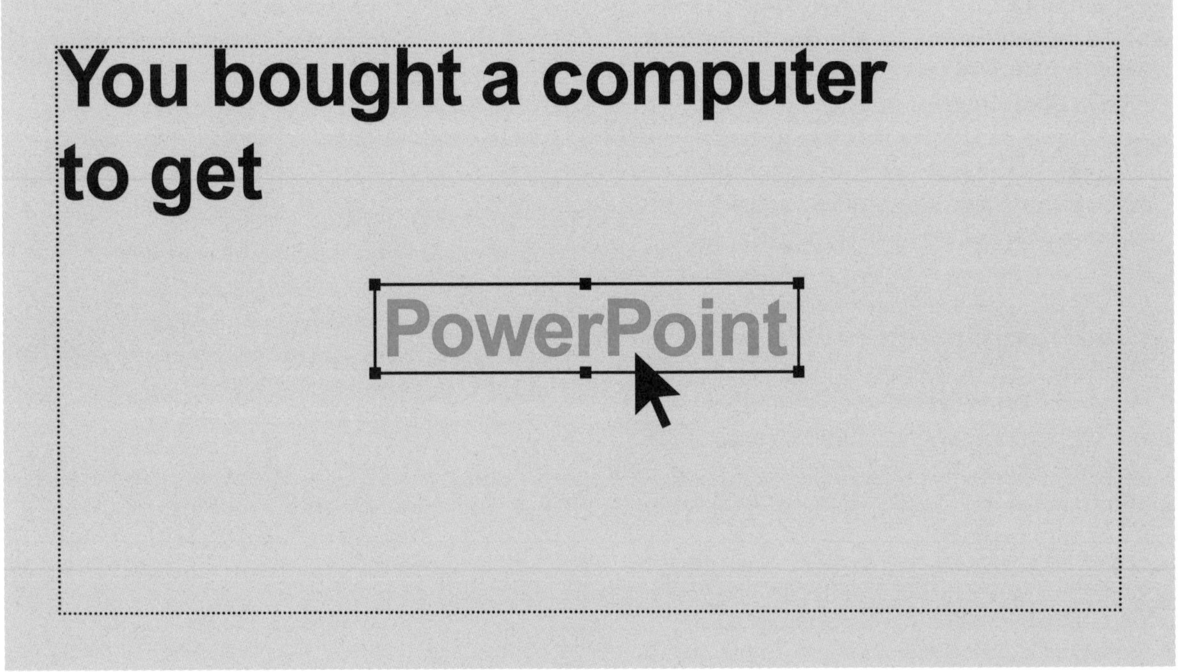
You bought a computer
to get
PowerPoint

Gaskins understood the unique power of such a tool and he had the skills and determination to make it happen. He saw that the point-and-click, Graphical User Interface world could enable this tool. He wasn't side-tracked by the 'outliner' philosophy – he knew that direct control of visual design was important. He built a diverse team that understood the cultures it was enabling.

All of which made PowerPoint a massive success.

It's hard to imagine now but in the 1980s PowerPoint was so striking and powerful that people would buy expensive computer systems just to get it. It was why businesses bought computers. Especially computers with fancy graphic capabilities. Until PowerPoint came along many business people couldn't imagine needing a computer that did anything more elaborate than show bright green text on a dark green screen.

PowerPoint gave colour screens, point and click, and nice-looking fonts a point. A powerful point.

But also...

It’s what everyone’s got
because it’s what everyone’s got

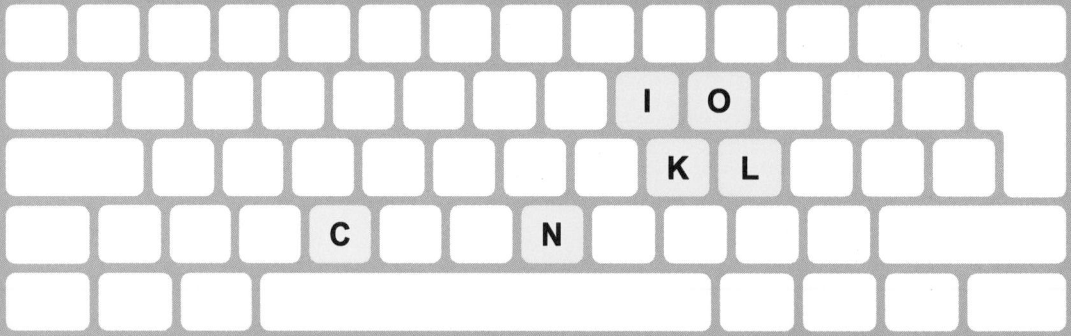

It's like QWERTY

There's a phenomenon called lock-in. With some products and technologies, once enough people are using it, it makes sense for everyone to use it. PowerPoint got off the ground to start with because it was a smart product that tapped into something real people wanted to do.

And after its initial success Microsoft used their marketing expertise* to make PowerPoint the default choice for businesses and organisations everywhere. PowerPoint got bundled with Office and it became the presentation software everyone had. That made it the lingua franca for organisations. If you sent someone a PowerPoint deck you would be pretty confident they could open it.

And Microsoft have been good stewards of PowerPoint's considerable historical legacy. They work very hard to make sure that it's backwards compatible. You can, for instance, open a PowerPoint 3.0 file from 1992 in today's version on an iPad Pro and all the animations will run as intended. This is extremely unusual in the software world and requires an enormous amount of effort on Microsoft's part.

But imagine if they didn't do it. Some vast proportion of the knowledge created in the last thirty years is now stored in old PowerPoint presentations. Losing that would be a loss of knowledge equivalent to the burning of the Library of Alexandria.†

* And their predatory exploitation of monopoly power in operating systems. Let's not forget that.

† I am aware that PowerPoint detractors would expect me to use inverted commas around the word 'knowledge' at this point. But what was in the Library of Alexandria? You're not telling me every scroll was a high-quality knowledge product. There must have been some vacuous mission statements in there.

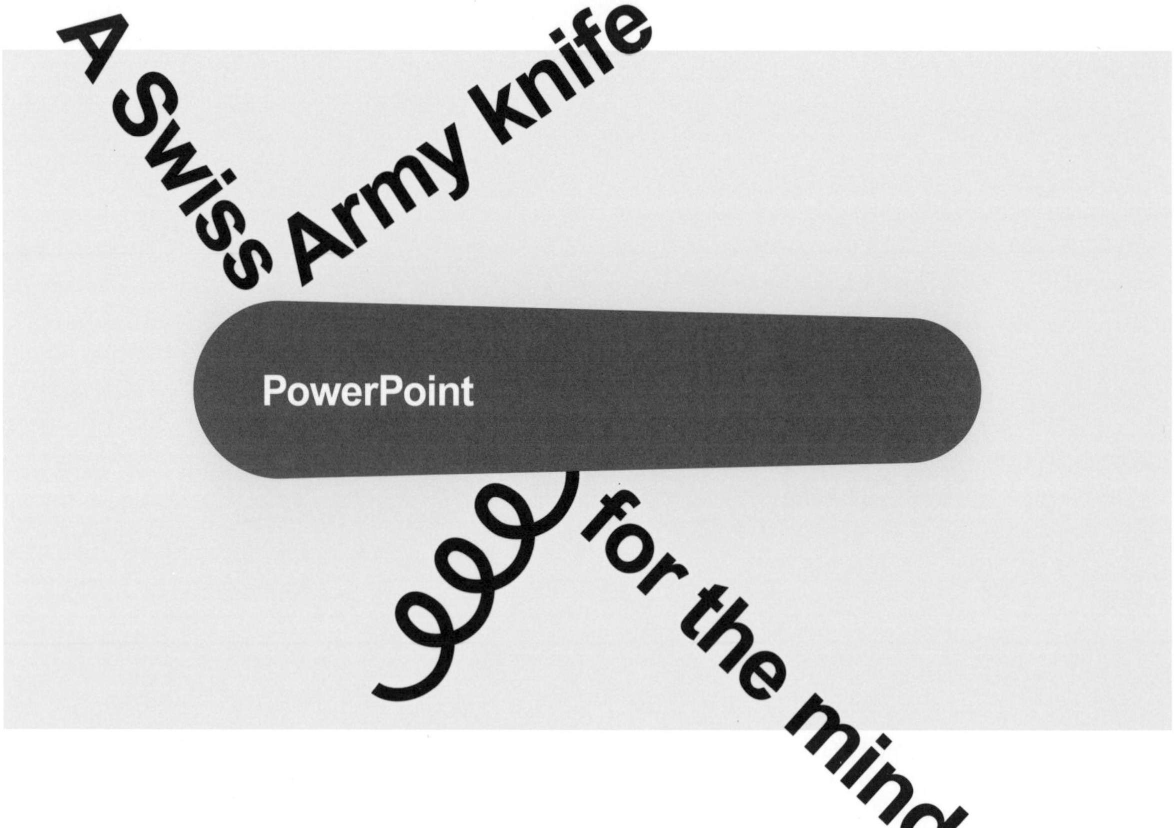
A Swiss Army knife
for the mind
PowerPoint

Stefanie Posavec is a designer and illustrator. (She designed this book. Thanks Stef!) I interviewed her for the *Wired* article about PowerPoint and she told me that the clients she works with all have one thing in common – PowerPoint.

> If you design something for somebody, they say 'I don't have a design program, I have PowerPoint. Can you make me a brochure that works in PowerPoint so I can change it? – because that's the only way that I know how to work with images.'

I asked the anthropologist and designer Georgina Voss to explain PowerPoint's success for the same article. She said this:

> PowerPoint has become the default for what a presentation is – more than just 'biro' or 'hoover' describing any ballpoint pen or vacuum cleaner, but actually moulding in its affordances and use behaviours such that using any non-PowerPoint program becomes more difficult. People in the Global North who have come through standard schooling and workplaces understand, broadly, how to use PowerPoint.

And Microsoft know people use PowerPoint for way more than presentations, so they always load it up with all the latest gubbins. You can do animation with it, you can retouch photos, it'll listen to your presentation and tell you not to swear so much. PowerPoint is your general purpose, do-it-all, DIY, whatever-you-want everything-store, Desert Island software. Don't leave home without it.

Steve Jobs famously claimed computers were the equivalent of bicycles for our minds. Powerful tools, but powerful because they were simple. He was equally famously dismissive of PowerPoint and of Microsoft. He thought they had no taste and were unable to make audaciously world-changing products because they couldn't strip things back to their irreducible core. He might have had a case. But PowerPoint is Microsoft's counterpoint: it's because they've thrown the kitchen sink in that it's taken over the world.

It’s got room for you and for pictures of your kids

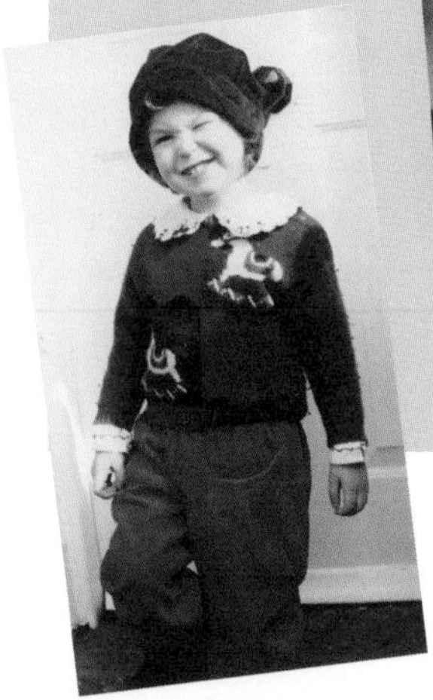

Katrina Sluis is a researcher and curator of art, images and computational culture. She thinks this is the basis of PowerPoint's appeal:

> It's therapeutic. I guess what's interesting about PowerPoint is it mixes the corporate business presentation with the possibility of creativity and the idea of personal expression. I think it offers just enough personal customisation for it to be seen as a creative act for many people. I wonder if that explains its persistence – the tension between the boring corporate aesthetics and the potential to put a slide of your children to nail your message home.

Sluis also believes PowerPoint has been surfing a cultural wave for the last thirty-plus years – the growing importance of the image:

> It's the arrival of visual speech, in a way, which you kind of see with the camera phone. And the way in which, in the attention economy, the image is reified. Images have a kind of rhetorical power now in contemporary culture.

We're living in a world made by Instagram, Snapchat and TikTok; we do not need to be convinced of the importance of the image in communication. But this wasn't obvious when the outliners argued for the primacy of the word in making presentation software. PowerPoint is as much about images as it is about words.

More interestingly, it's about combining the two. It's the software embodiment of one of the most significant movements in art. The Pulitzer Prize-winning poet Charles Simic will now explain:

> Collage, the art of reassembling fragments of pre-existing images in such a way as to form a new image, was the most important innovation in the art of the twentieth century.

He could have been talking about PowerPoint.

It tickles our brains in interesting ways

We saw Jennifer Egan's PowerPoint earlier in the book. She says this about it:

> It is not a flow. It is a series of images and moments.

It doesn't flow like music, cinema or the written word. It's not static like a painting. It's a series of images or moments. A bit like comics. But the pace is out of the control of the viewer. There's a person in there too. It's a three-way dance: the audience, the presenter, the slides.

So all sorts of interesting things happen when we look at a series of slides.

Our brains love to solve puzzles and find connections. They'll find meaning even if there isn't any there (this is called apophenia). Like the way we see faces in clouds. A series of images is exactly what this instinct likes to feed on. We're hungry for those connections. Make a minimal effort to ensure those connections actually exist and you've got our brains gripped.

Effective slides also tap into some of our neural biases because a great slide is often a striking new metaphor. Our brains light up like a classroom of kids with laser pointers.

Will Storr talks about this in his book *The Science of Storytelling*:

> Brain scans illustrate the second, more powerful, use of metaphor. When participants in one study read the words 'he had a rough day', their neural regions involved in feeling textures became more activated, compared with those who read 'he had a bad day'.

PowerPoint encourages us to create metaphors by combining words and pictures to say the same thing.

Brains like that. It's even how we daydream. As George Eliot put it in *Middlemarch*:

> Our moods are apt to bring with them images which succeed each other like the magic-lantern pictures of a doze.

They love it even more when there are people involved.

It’s
Soylent
Green

PowerPoint is people

So why do presentations work better than memos? (Often, not always – we'll get to that.) If it's about the combination of words and pictures why doesn't that work in a document? If it's about the combined performance of presenter, slides and pictures, why is it so much less compelling on video? Why do presentations work?

It's because PowerPoint is made out of people.

It's a neurological, psychological, evolutionary fact that we're interested in other people. We're drawn to them, to watch them and to work out what they want and what they're up to. The best art manages to convince us that we're in the presence of a person. Elegant craft, such as deep empathetic writing or film-making, somehow sustains the illusion that a real living human has been conjured into life. PowerPoint doesn't have to bother, it just plonks a real person right there in front of us.

And they're live. They're right there, happening right now. So we watch for the same reason that we watch Formula One. It's mostly dreary and predictable but at any moment something extraordinary might happen.

And the conversational style of a good presentation helps too. It's not a speech, it's not radio, it's structured but conversational. It seems designed to 'go in' in just the right way.

The cognitive scientist Laura Mickes once wrote this about the style of writing you get on social media:

> The relatively unfiltered and spontaneous production of one person's mind is just the sort of thing that is readily stored in another's mind.

That seems to capture the best of PowerPoint too. It's like a great conversation but with pictures and without the need for tedious small talk.

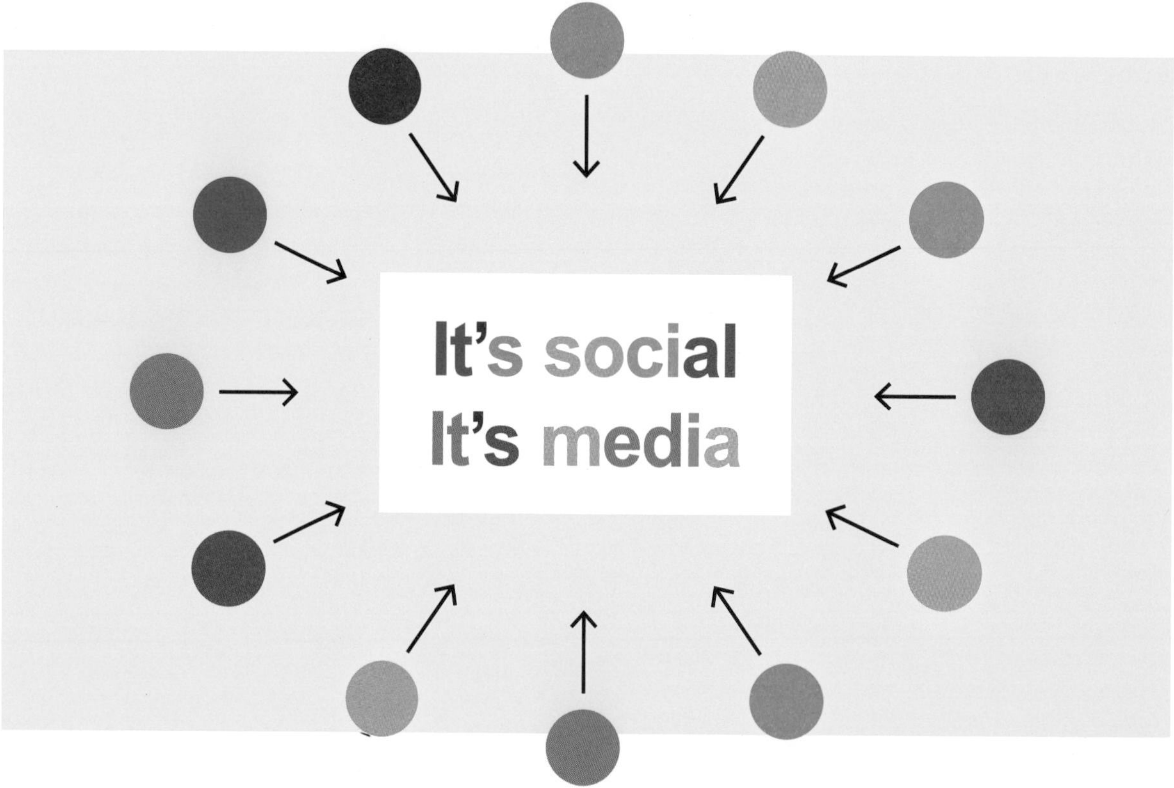
It's social
It's media

Robert knew this

This was something that Robert Gaskins spotted. PowerPoint isn't just a social tool at the point of use, when you're doing a presentation. It's often also social at the point of production.

A PowerPoint presentation is frequently a team effort and it's very often important. It's a pitch, a chance to make a case, bidding for budget approval or for the opportunity to do something bigger or better. It's the team collaborating on something that matters. This is where relationships get built or undermined, where growth and learning happens. Writing a deck inside an organisation is half being gathered round the campfire and half being trapped in a foxhole. Gaskins says:

> The 'social' aspect of PowerPoint usage is often totally invisible to academics and consultants, who use PowerPoint all by themselves to produce material for a more effective personal performance, and for whom higher production values take on a dominating importance.

Doing this well is a superpower for organisations. You can use it to get all sorts of people and teams aligned. Advertising agencies cohere around big pitches to prospective clients; start-ups find their mission and the language to describe it through the iterative pitches they have to create for venture capitalists.

Remember the Scandi-noir TV feast *The Bridge*? Every now and then the two main detectives would instruct each other to 'think out loud'. They'd talk and a new way forward would pop out. That's what writing a presentation can do for your team.

Many of the formative moments at the Government Digital Service were when we had to come together to craft our message to be presented to other departments. I got a lot of my enthusiasm for simple, plain clarity in those meetings. If you can get to something clear and cogent when you're working with each other you can be powerful and persuasive when you're presenting to the people who can sign off your budgets.

It sparks

joy

This is what everyone forgets

The PowerPoint grouches, the people who tell us it's killing thought and bankrupting businesses, they all forget that making a PowerPoint deck is about the most fun a knowledge worker can have without being OOO.

Noodling over just what font to choose is pleasing. Aligning boxes is satisfying. Sanding a sprawling list of blah blah blah down to a tight five principles lights up our pleasure centres. And then we get to choose the pictures. And draw a clever little diagram. And throw in a GIF.

We do it because we like it.

And that's also why we do it well. In many organisational lives PowerPoint is where the creativity and satisfaction sits. Not the big creativity of architects and corporate art but the small, everyday folk creativity we get from handicraft and crosswords and a tiny job well done.

So much of modern business life is like *Tetris*. Email, chat, Slack, everything. You complete a line and more stuff just comes at you. A presentation also offers the special pleasure of being completable. A PowerPoint deck can be finished. You can tick it off. A presentation happens and then you can move on.

Joyce Carol Oates advises new writers to look for things they can complete:

> Short stories, monologues, poetry, things that you can finish and show other people. That's very satisfying and necessary for a writer. What we all need is the satisfaction of this little uplift that we get psychologically from finishing something.

We could add PowerPoint to that list. That's what it does for us.

The formalising power of rectangles

Also, let's face it, there's just something powerful about rectangles.

Artists know this. So do film directors. Put an image inside a rectangular box and we relate to it differently.

We've learned that this image now embodies some meaning, that some artistic, creative decisions have been made. This image, this crop, this size, these colours. They all mean something and we react to that meaning even if we don't think about it.

PowerPoint gets us to think inside the box.

> ‘Art is how we decorate space, music is how we decorate time.’
>
> **Jean-Michel Basquiat**

PowerPoint is how we decorate both

Humans are communicators. We’re social. It’s why we have big brains and it’s what’s made us the only species on the planet capable of fucking the whole thing up. It shouldn’t be a big surprise that a bit of software specifically designed to let us communicate that way – via all available channels – has been a big success.

PowerPoint was designed, from the get-go, to integrate reading, talking and showing pictures. It pretty quickly added sound. It does not, as yet, integrate smell and taste, but there are probably some boffins at Microsoft’s Making PowerPoint Even More Dominant Division working on it.

All human life is there. And yet, and yet. Some people just can’t stand it.

"People who know what they're talking about don't need PowerPoint."

– Steve Jobs

Speaking truth to PowerPoint

We met Edward Tufte earlier in the book. He's a hero of mine. He makes this point about PowerPoint:

> The evidence indicates that PowerPoint, compared to other common presentation tools, reduces the analytical quality of serious presentations of evidence. This is especially the case for the PowerPoint ready-made templates, which corrupt statistical reasoning, and often weaken verbal and spatial thinking.

He's right. Organisational cultures get obsessed with PowerPoint and they use it for everything. Lots of the time this is fine, but there are instances when it isn't. PowerPoint is not optimised for the visualisation of precise and detailed engineering data. And this, particularly, is what Tufte was concerned about. In his famous polemic 'PowerPoint does Rocket Science' he places blame for the Space Shuttle Columbia disaster on the use of PowerPoint to present technical information.

He's basically saying, don't do a presentation

His recommendation is that, for 'serious presentations', PowerPoint be dropped and replaced with word-processing or page-layout software. He suggests Word. So, practically, what he's proposing is that someone writes a good and effective document (a memo, a piece of prose), which everyone reads.

> Replacing PowerPoint with Microsoft Word (or, better, a tool with non-proprietary universal formats) will make presentations and their audiences smarter. Of course full-screen projected images and videos are necessary; that is the one harmless use of PP. Meetings should center on concisely written reports on paper, not fragmented bulleted talking points projected up on the wall.

Amazon agree.

Amazon CEO Jeff Bezos says:

> Many, many years ago, we outlawed PowerPoint presentations at Amazon … it's probably the smartest thing we ever did.

Instead meetings at Amazon start with everyone sitting and reading a 'six-page, narratively structured memo' for about the first thirty minutes of the meeting.

If you read Bezos's Annual Letters to shareholders you'll know that he's either a great writer or a serial hirer of great ghosts. He prefers memos, he says, because each has 'verbs and sentences and topic sentences and complete paragraphs'. He obviously values the clarity and focus you get from a well-written, well-thought-through corporate document. And he knows that doing them well means giving them time and attention.

> The great memos are written and re-written, shared with colleagues who are asked to improve the work, set aside for a couple of days, and then edited again with a fresh mind … They simply can't be done in a day or two.
>
> [It] is harder for the author, but it forces the author to clarify their own thinking … it totally revolutionizes the way we do meetings at Amazon.

And it's not just Bezos. Many people have famously 'banned PowerPoint' from their organisations: Elon Musk, Mark Cuban, Jack Dorsey, Brigadier General H. R. McMaster. Mostly billionaires and generals. Mostly men. It's a list of people who don't have to work hard to get people to pay attention. And who might be impatient with underlings talking instead of them.

Robert Gaskins is also a fan of memos

As he said in an interview with the *Wall Street Journal*:

> A lot of people in business have given up writing the documents. They just write the presentations, which are summaries without

the detail, without the backup. A lot of people don't like the intellectual rigor of actually doing the work.

He was never guilty of that himself. The original business plan for PowerPoint was fifty-three densely worded pages, with a dozen accompanying slides.

This brings us to an important point: presentations and documents are not interchangeable. Sometimes you need the rigour and clarity of prose. And one of the downsides of PowerPoint's ubiquity is that people default to it. They will bash out some bullet points when they should be sitting, thinking and writing down a solid argument.

Personally, I think this presentation/document confusion is the most pernicious and alarming thing that PowerPoint has done. Bad presentations are normally bad because they should have been documents. And vice versa. It's just that in a time-pressed modern organisation people don't have the space to do both well. So you end up with ugly hybrids. We've all lived through presentations like that. Paragraphs of text on the screen, vast spreadsheets pasted into a document at a tiny size.

(Nancy Duarte, the presentation genius behind 'An Inconvenient Truth' and a thousand other great PowerPoints, is trying to solve this problem through the invention of Slidedocs. They're written documents, designed to be read, but created in presentation software and leaning on the visual tools you get from PowerPoint.)

So let's agree that, here and now. Not everything should be a presentation. Sometimes you need something else.

But let's also critique the critique

The anti-PowerPoint lobby shouldn't have it all their own way. There are other things going on here, elements of power preservation, myopia about privilege and old-fashioned, old-school, old-man-shouting-at-cloudisms.

One reason Bezos gave for the move to memos was this:

> We were doing the more traditional thing … a junior executive comes in, they put a huge amount of effort into developing a PowerPoint presentation, they put the third slide up, and the most senior executive in the room has already interrupted them, thrown them off their game, asking questions about what is going to be presented in slide six, if they would just stay quiet for a moment…

You didn't have to invent a whole new way of doing meetings to fix that. You could just be polite.

Eugene Wei, an investor, technologist and talented blogger, used to work for Bezos. He suggests that much of the shift to memos is down to

> just how much it mattered to Bezos to be able to consume the content at his own pace. In the lead-up to the switch from PowerPoint to memos, I sat in many a meeting where someone would be going through a slide deck for Jeff and he had already skipped ahead in the printed copy to some much later slide. That pacing problem would visibly frustrate him.

Again, there's a simple fix. Be more patient.

I'm being petty. But there's a bigger point here. Meetings aren't just about the exchange of information. They're also about power. (They're mostly about power.) And if the meeting has been designed solely to meet the informational requirements of one person, or one organisational caste, then you might have a bigger problem.

The power is the point

Tufte does something similar in his essay 'The Cognitive Style of PowerPoint' when he talks about Louis Gerstner becoming president of IBM. Gerstner decided to rid IBM of their dependence on presentations and instead said to people, 'Let's just talk about your business.'

> And then Gerstner later asked IBM executives to write out their business strategies in longhand using the presentation methodology of sentences, with subjects and predicates, nouns and verbs, which then combine sequentially to form paragraphs, an analytic tool demonstratively better than slideware bullet lists.
>
> 'Let's just talk about your business' indicates a thoughtful exchange of information, a mutual interplay between speaker and audience, rather than a pitch made by a power pointer pointing to bullets. PowerPoint is presenter-oriented, not content-oriented, not audience-oriented. PP advertising is not about content quality, but rather presenter therapy.

This feels like it's written by someone who's used to being listened to, someone who's never had to ask for attention. Someone with power.

This appeal, 'let's just talk about your business', is the kind of folksy request that seems all friendly on the surface but is freighted with significance when you think about power.

It reminds me of Jo Freeman's legendary essay 'The Tyranny of Structurelessness', a look at power relations within radical feminist collectives but equally applicable when anyone powerful in an organisation tries to suggest everyone should 'just chat'.

> This apparent lack of structure too often disguised an informal, unacknowledged and unaccountable leadership that was all the more pernicious because its very existence was denied.

Tufte is designing for a world where organisational life is full of mutually supportive peers, all equally empowered to thoughtfully exchange information and all clear on what a predicate is. That's not been my experience.

He's also rather contemptuous of the way PowerPoint is explicitly designed to be helpful to presenters, dismissing it as 'presenter therapy'. This is the criticism I dislike the most.

Fight the power

If you're a CEO, a general, or a renowned academic; or charismatic, outgoing and articulate; or a tall able-bodied white man, you might not need PowerPoint.

You're probably good at public speaking and even if you're not, people are going to listen. Because they have to. And you may well find other people's use of PowerPoint annoying. Why can't they just leave out the bits you disagree with or already know? Why can't they speak with the fluency and authority you do?

Bully for them, I guess. But most of us aren't those people. PowerPoint is for us. It's training wheels for public speaking. It gets us up and running. PowerPoint makes presenting seem possible for people who aren't brimming with the confidence of privilege. People who are underrepresented in public life. Women. People of colour. People with disabilities.

Many of the anti-PowerPointers seem to be arguing for a return to 'speeches'. Slideless, meandering talks with nothing to look at but a dreary individual who's decided to abandon their notes and just wing it. There's a good reason that a speech these days looks as odd as someone walking in front of your car with a red flag. It's rubbish.

Say what you like about PowerPoint – at least it makes someone think about the topic before they stand up and talk. They've at least had to write some slides and decide on a title and one of the slides has to be the last one – so there will be, at least theoretically – an end.

None of these guarantees exist in the world of unstructured, slide-free public speaking. The best public speakers might still be brilliant, with PowerPoint or without. But the vast majority would get horribly worse.

Speaking in public is intimidating. It's even worse when you don't have a supportive infrastructure like PowerPoint. Even the professionals who are supposed to be good at it are surprisingly bad.

The only reason they think their presentations are more entertaining than PowerPoint is that they don't have to hear themselves talk.

Banning PowerPoint would result in a net reduction in the quantity, quality and diversity of public speech.

Fortunately, it's not going anywhere

We will get rid of PowerPoint just after we get rid of QWERTY.

There is a lot of very solid and well-researched evidence that suggests that the QWERTY keyboard layout is a terrible way to input text into a machine. And that this hangover from the days of typewriting is a legacy that must be abandoned if we want to achieve maximal productivity. Many people will engage you about this issue if you let them.

It's not going to happen though, is it? QWERTY is what we've got. We're not going to embrace DVORAK or chording or anything else.

We're just going to learn to type and get on with things.

Same goes for PowerPoint. It's what we've got. We may as well get good at it.

The rest of this book is designed to help you do that.

PART THREE

PowerPoint is Easy

Make it big
Keep it short
Have a point

OK. Disclaimer. I'm a little uncomfortable about the rest of this book.

I've read tons of books about presenting and presentations and most of them just make me nervous. Partly because they tend to be really complicated and prescriptive (you must do this, you must do that) and partly because they spend their whole time telling you to relax. Which just makes people anxious.

And I'm about to do both of those things.

So before we get into it can I just say this?

This is just my experience.

As we've previously established, I'm a tall white man. I'm also straight, able-bodied, cis, gentile and neurotypical with a good job and a supportive family. I've learned to present in circumstances of tremendous privilege. I have no idea whether the advice in here will work for you. I've written it with some firmness and authority because it reads better like that, but really it's all hedged around with doubt and ambiguity.

What follows is a big old pile of things that have worked for me. Loosely divided up into sections on words, design and performance. They're intended as inspiration, not instruction. You'll see that I follow my own advice and repeat myself quite a lot, but I try and do it in different ways each time. So some of the advice is a single slide, some of it is a bit more involved.

If there's a single theme to all this advice it's this: make it shorter. Tighter. More compact. Most of the advice in this book boils down to that. Because it's hard to do.

I have proof.

In April 2021 *Nature* published a paper called 'People systematically overlook subtractive changes'. It described how, when confronted with a problem, people's natural tendency is to solve it by adding things rather than taking things away. They demonstrated this with a bunch of different experiments and scenarios. For instance, when asked to straighten out an unbalanced Lego structure people immediately think about adding bricks, not removing them, even when taking them away would have been quicker and easier.

Anyone who has to make things that communicate will tell you how true this is. That's why the creative industries are full of people whose job it is to remove things. To dispassionately and expertly go through someone else's work and take stuff out. Editors. Sub-editors. Producers. Curators. Agents. Gallerists. DJs. They cut away the fluff and get to the essence.

When you do your presentation you probably won't have someone like that to help you. So think of the next section as something like that. It's a series of techniques to help you make your presentation short and effective. And to give you a bit of confidence in it.

The 48 Laws of

1. Don't just read the screen
2. Lists
3. Use lists
4. Lots of lists
5. But 48 items is way too many – who thought this was a good idea?
6. Start with a story
7. End with an ask
8. Fill up the rest with ideas and images
9. Repeat the important things
10. Remove the word 'key'
11. Make it shorter
12. Repeat the important things
13. Don't just read the screen
14. Arrive early
15. Respect the AV people
16. Be a bit bigger
17. Make it clear, concise and catchy
18. Or freewheeling, unpredictable and magical
19. Just be sure which one you're doing
20. Repeat the important things
21. Arrive early
22. Double-check the tech
23. What will you do if your slides don't work?
24. Press B

PowerPoint

25. Make something very big
26. Make something very small
27. Make something rhyme
28. Finish on time
29. Actually, finish early
30. Never outshine the master
31. Sorry, wrong list
32. One hour of prep per one minute of talk
33. Repeat the important things
34. Demand change
35. Make it readable
36. Make it accessible
37. Make it memorable
38. Make it bigger
39. Remove the word 'holistic'
40. No 3D
41. No pies
42. Slow down
43. Speed up
44. Repeat the important things
45. Start with a story
46. End with a bang
47. Don't just read the screen
48. BANG

Use words
Not too many
Mostly short

Don't aim for excellence; excellence will screw you up and get in your head.

Lower the bar. Just avoid mistakes.

Just do these seven things:

Divide your presentation into three sections.
Make your words short, big and clear.
Make your pictures relevant, big and clear.
Don't have many colours.
Don't have many fonts.
Practise a lot.
Be yourself.

This will get you an excellent presentation.
You don't have to be Steve Jobs.

Honestly, those  will do. But if you'd like more…

Don’t begin at the beginning

> You know that Chinese proverb, 'A journey of a thousand miles starts with a single step'? Turns out, if we were contemplating a thousand-mile walk, we'd be better off imagining ourselves looking back from the destination and figuring how we got there. When it comes to advance thinking, standing at the end and looking backward is much more effective than looking forward from the beginning.
>
> Annie Duke, *Thinking in Bets: Making Smarter Decisions When You Don't Have All the Facts*

The hardest and most important thing to get right in any presentation is the end. That's when you have to close the deal, make the ask. That's when people are going to be paying the most attention. The Peak End Rule is a psychological effect that suggests that people tend to judge an experience by how it feels at its most intense moment and at its end, rather than by the totality of the thing. Our memories of an experience are overly dictated by the end.

Many people get this wrong. They start well but the end just peters out, or they don't even get there, because they've run out of time. That's normally because they do the end last. They sit down to write their presentation, start with the start and have run out of energy or ideas by the time they get to the end.

Apparently John le Carré once met Agatha Christie at a party and asked her how she devised her elegant murderous plots.* She explained that it was easy. She just wrote down most of the story without any real idea of who the murderer was going to be, figured out who the reader would think was most unlikely and then went back and changed the story so it was, in fact, them. You can do the same thing.

It's also one of Pixar's storytelling rules:

> Endings are hard, get yours working up front.

* I heard this story on the *Rule Of Three* podcast. The Lucy Porter episode. I've not been able to track down any other evidence of the truth of this but that'll do for you, won't it? It seems true, right?

Change is possible

PointFul

You get your ending by getting clear about what it is you're asking for. What change are you demanding from your audience? Work that out and make sure you ask them. Don't just do an 'update'. What are you trying to achieve?

As leading speechwriter Peggy Noonan will tell you in her book *On Speaking Well*:

> Every speech has a job to do, and no matter who you are, pope, president, poet or pipe layer, if you're giving a speech you have to understand what its job is and work to make sure it's done.

This is your opportunity to ask for something that will make the world slightly better. You might as well take it. Otherwise what is the point?

(Even if your boss just asks you do an 'update', it will be much more effective if you frame it as an 'ask'. Tell everyone what you've been up to and then suggest something be done differently. Your presentation will seem, and be, much more pointful.)

Make your ending your ask. And during the course of your presentation supply enough information to make that ask seem entirely reasonable. Easy.

☐ Beginning

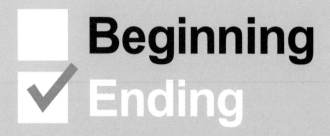

☑ Ending

You already know the end – the beginning is now easy.

If you genuinely can't think of anything else, you could just tell people what you're going to say at the end. That's a valid technique. No one's coming to a work meeting for a big twist, they're not hoping for M. Night Shyamalan.

Or you can cleverly allude to it. Tease the ending a bit and hint at where you might be going. This is a very popular trick with newspaper columnists – as long as the first and last sentences contain an echo of each other, people are convinced of the coherence of the whole thing. It makes you look very smart.

As Sam Leith says in *Write to the Point*:

> Closing where you opened doesn't cost much mental energy [...] and the payoff can be considerable. Even if what's in between is a bit of a ramble, the sense of closure it brings will leave your readers with the impression of something neat and well-made.

This is true of every piece of writing. And most creative endeavours. They call it a reprise in music. Or the recapitulation. Keep going to the end of the book to see if I remember to do it.

- [x] Beginning
- [ ] Jokes, images, facts and stories
- [x] Ending

You've got an end. Now you just need to fill it up with jokes, stories, images and facts that help you make your point.

I know that seems incredibly reductionist and banal but that's all you need to do.

In this context 'jokes' means just behave like you normally would when you're talking to people. Don't be artificially funny. Don't be artificially unfunny. The playwright and genius Ken Campbell used to say that most drama was unrealistic because it didn't have jokes in it, and real life has jokes. Be Like Ken. Don't shoehorn humour in, but don't be weirdly po-faced and professional either.

Images should be self-explanatory. We'll have a bit more on that later.

Facts. I hope you've got some facts. I know this book is all about 'surface' and presentation but facts are an astoundingly effective way to persuade people to do stuff. A fact per slide is a good rule of thumb. It will also increase your confidence if your presentation contains a lot of unassailable real-world factitude – if you're trying to get by on rhetoric you'll never escape that gnawing feeling in your stomach. And the most compelling facts are new ones. If you teach your audience something they don't already know, they'll love you and remember you.

And then there's stories. Do not be alarmed and intimidated by all the 'story' talk out there. Within your presentation it's just helpful and persuasive if you talk about things that you or other real people have actually done. People remember people and what they do. If you're too abstract for too long they'll get lost. So, every now and then, you should start a sentence with 'I did this' or 'We found this' or 'It's a bit like when we all…'. Describe a moment or an event where something tangible and comprehensible happened to a real person. Ideally yourself. We call these things 'stories' but they don't have to be life-changing narratives with the tension and power of a Norse myth. Just some stuff that's happened to some people.

If you have a good beginning, a good ending, you're clear what you're asking for and you've got a series of jokes, images, facts and stories which all drive towards that ask, then you're good to go. You'll do a great presentation.

HOWEVER, lots of people get worried at this point. They find it difficult to marshall all the material and work out what order to put it in. This is often when they'll turn to presentation advice in books or on the internet. And, once again, 'story' will rear its forbidding head. Because they'll often tell you that the essence of a good presentation is a good story. And that it should have this or that elemental, universal structure. The Hero's Journey or Save the Cat or Freytag's Pyramid.

They're not *wrong* about these things. But it's not very helpful. Making your whole presentation into a single, coherent story is very tricky. (Making a popular television series or movie into a single, coherent story is frequently beyond the wit of many professional screenwriters, so what chance do you have?)

So just don't worry about it.

You don't need to figure out who the hero of your Q4 Financial Results is or what the inciting incident in your fundraising report was. Just divide your presentation into three.

There are three good reasons for this:

1. Ninety per cent of the time it'll work. Most good creative/communications things are, basically, in three parts.

2. It'll make you think about it. You won't just do a huge splurge of content. You'll have some structure and that's most of the battle.

3. It'll get you there quickly. It's one less choice and one more constraint. This is always useful.

☑ Beginning

- ☐ **Section 1**
  Jokes, images, facts and stories
- ☐ **Section 2**
  Jokes, images, facts and stories
- ☐ **Section 3**
  Jokes, images, facts and stories

☑ Ending

number Three, that's the magic

What does it all mean?

De La Soul weren't just the progenitors of Daisy Age hip-hop – they also neatly summarised an important insight about human and corporate communication.

Management consultants do it all the time. McKinsey consultants, especially, are trained to answer most questions with, 'There are three reasons. Firstly ... Secondly ... Thirdly...'

It makes you seem certain and analytical. People can remember those reasons and debate them, and it gives you something to do with your hands. (Always count your reasons off on your fingers.)

In his book *First You Write a Sentence*, Joe Moran suggests that the power of three goes very deep:

> Perhaps it is because three is the smallest number with a rhythm. Rhythm is not just the beat but the spaces between the beat – so you need at least two spaces, and hence three beats, to create it. With three things, you can set up a pattern, then break it. Tension is created, built and resolved. A quest story has three narrative phases: departure, adventure, return. Jokes have a set-up, reiteration and punchline. A twelve-bar-blues singer sings a first line, repeats it and then improvises a third, longer line.

The Economist is famous for its ability to make you feel like you understand abstruse and difficult topics. One of the ways they do it is by littering their pages with Three Reasons for everything.

Zanny Minton Beddoes, the editor, was asked why they do this. She cited brevity: 'I find journalistically articles that have very long lists of reasons just very heavy going'; structure: 'I attach huge importance to the structure of an argument, I think it's really important that an argument is made clearly'; and discipline: 'Three reasons is a function of thinking through the structure of an argument. That's a really important discipline to be able to make your argument clearly.'

For example:

Flora Joll is an advertising and communications strategist. This is a slide/structure she used for a recent pitch. It's perfect. You know where you're going, you're in safe hands.

Songwriter Harlan Howard described a great country song as 'three chords and the truth'. That's what this is. A big overarching theme (What's the one thing you've got to say?) and that truth told in three parts.

You'll find that many presentations are boring because they're just divided in two: Problem and Solution. To maintain some interest you need three bits – crisis, struggle, resolution. Three little pigs is drama. Two little pigs is an anecdote.

It's simple. It works. And it's helpful and clarifying to decide, before you start, that you're going to do it in three sections. It's one less thing to worry about.

You still have to think about it. You still have to marshal your arguments and get your facts into a coherent order. But if you decide, from the beginning, that it's going to be divided into three you'll remove many options and make your life much easier.

A brutal start, a cheerier ending

For instance:

Last quarter
This quarter
Next quarter

Problem
Solution
Next steps

Exposition
Complication
Resolution

Content
Strategy
Tactics

Analysis
Diagnosis
Actions

Beginning
Middle
End

Customers
Competitors
Category

Story of self
Story of us
Story of now

Past
Present
Future

Mission
Values
Culture

Where we've been
Where we are now
Where we're going

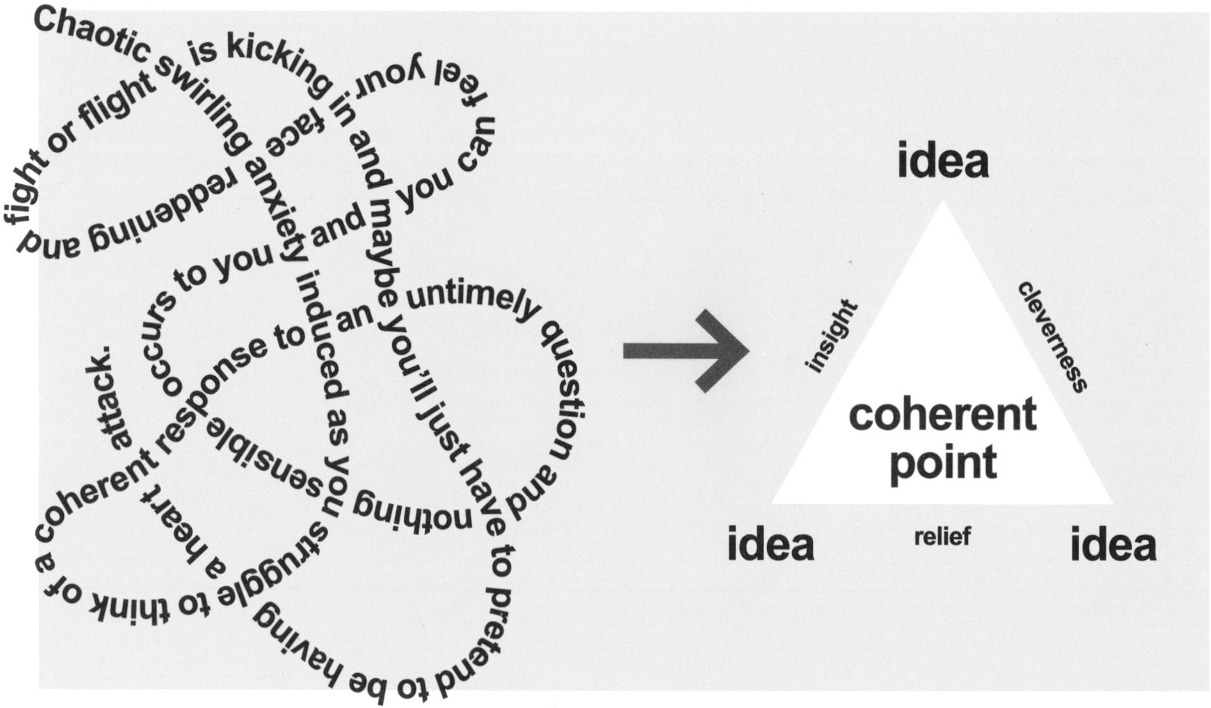
Chaotic swirling anxiety induced as you struggle to think of a coherent response to an untimely question and nothing sensible occurs to you and you can feel your face reddening and fight or flight is kicking in and maybe you'll just have to pretend to be having a heart attack.
idea
insight
cleverness
coherent point
idea
relief
idea

Practically, though…

A great way to think about this is to get your notebook or whiteboard, draw a triangle and start planning out your presentation like that. The three sides can be your main points, the centre can be the title. Or the three points could be your points (ha!) and the sides are the connecting ideas between them. Getting it down into a simple graphic like this can be a big help.

(This is also a great technique if you find yourself in a situation where you need to improvise a strategy. Start by wandering over to the whiteboard, or by grabbing a napkin, and then draw a triangle. You immediately look like you know what you're doing. Then you just start breaking the problem down into threes. People will be bowled over.)*

* My friend Dylan Williams taught me this trick. Thanks, Dylan.

‘We should torture language to tell the truth.’

Rachel Kushner,
The Flamethrowers

We have an end. We have a beginning. We have some stuff to put in the middle. We've divided all that up into three. Our battle now is to make all our actual words clear, concise and catchy. We want to be understood and remembered. This, again, is easy, it just takes a bit of work. We have to poke at the words a bit. Bash them around to extract our truth from the corporate miasma. But it's not inherently difficult and there are some simple tricks that will help us out.

Just remove the word 'key'

Organisational life is full of words that have lost all meaning. Their sense has been rubbed off. Get rid of them.

You have some 'Key Objectives'. Fine. Have you got any other Objectives? Some non-key ones? Probably not. So no meaning will be lost if you remove the word 'key'. On your first encounter with any corporate document just go through and take the keys out. While you're at it you'll realise that there are a ton of other words you could lose too. 'Holistic', for instance. No one knows what that means. Take it out. Or 'engagement'. Or 'evolve'. People use 'evolve' as a fancy way to say 'change'. But change is fine. Unless you actually do mean 'subject to generations of random mutation and fitness tests leading to unpredictable new forms'.

Removing these words gets you warmed up. It sharpens your knife for the real work ahead.

I know this sounds awfully pedantic. Like some dreadful old buffer complaining that television is an ugly neologism of Greek and Latin roots. I love the fact that language evolves (ha!). But what we're trying to do here is pay close attention to our words and strip out anything that isn't working really hard. That means being precise and careful. Removing 'key' is a great way to start.

(I learned to excise 'key' from the magnificent Sarah Richards. She was Head of Content Design at GDS and has a very low tolerance for this kind of flummery. She is one of the major reasons UK services like 'replacing your driving licence' are now so straightforward and nonsense-free.)

WOULD
CUSTOMERS
PLEASE NOTE
THAT MARKET &
FOOD HALLS ARE
OPEN AS NORMAL

Then get rid of almost everything else

I am a bad person. An irritating pedant. I know that. But I can't help looking at a sign like this and getting cross. So many useless words. Noticing this kind of superfluity is just an annoying habit I have. But it comes in useful when I'm writing a presentation.

Why would you need to say 'would customers please note'? What does that add?

If you weren't a customer would it be any less true? And 'note'? Really? Like, write it down somewhere? In my book of Which Things Are Open As Normal?

And then there's 'Open As Normal', which suddenly raises the spectre of Abnormal Opening, something you hadn't previously considered. Abnormal Opening will presumably lead to Lovecraftian nightmares oozing from a blood-soaked wormhole. You don't want that.

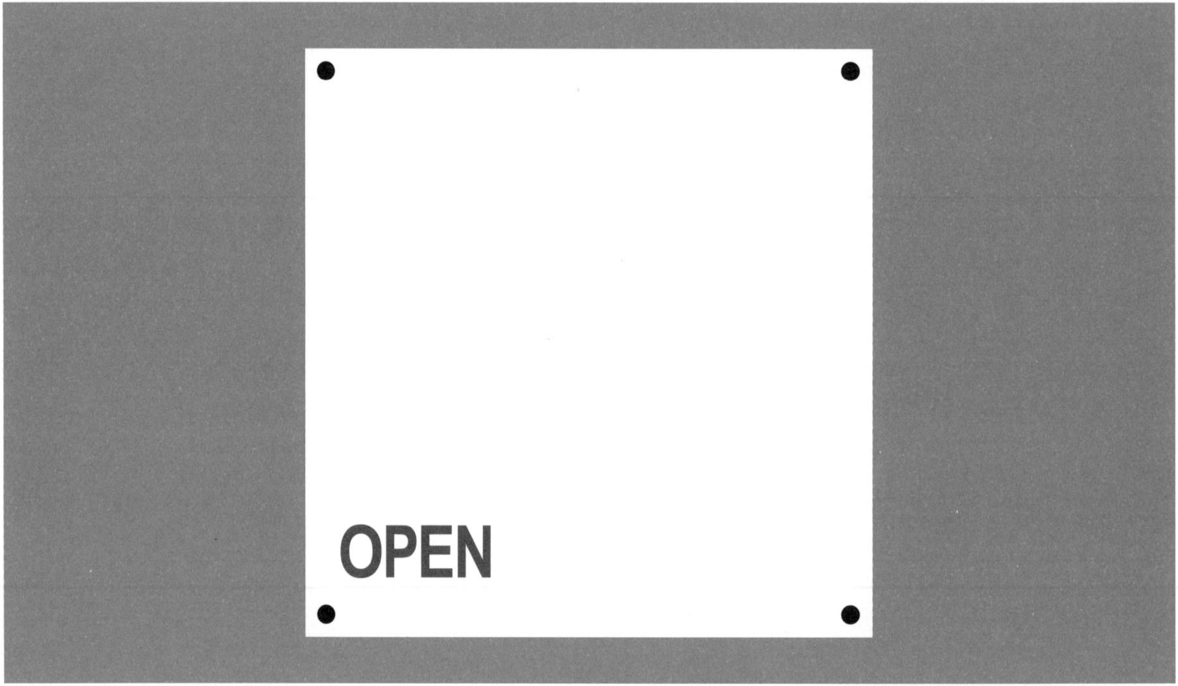
OPEN

Writing is thinking

We might start absorbing speech in the womb but we start ingesting corporate blah the minute we leave. So when we need to write something public or official we adopt it like we're dragging on a hi-vis vest or a business suit. We just feel, somehow, that this is how you're supposed to do it.

But you don't have to write that way. Not in email. Not when you're complaining to the council. Especially not when you're writing a presentation. It'll be too long, too vague and it won't stick in anyone's head.

I was once asked to write some presentation guidelines for the Government Digital Service. I think people were expecting the usual thing – put your name and title on the first slide, put a logo bottom right, no swearing, have a graduated blue background.

Instead I used the opportunity to get very involved with the presentations people wrote. To encourage big type and short words. To eliminate jargon and Three-Letter Acronyms. To get us saying what we actually meant. I think this helped us in our mission. People knew what we were saying, even if they didn't like it. And you could read our presentations if you happened to be sat at the back of the room.

I also think it made us strategically sharper, better aligned and intellectually more coherent. It's often in the process of writing external presentations that an organisation works out what it actually thinks. You normally get this kind of thing approved by writing corporate blah. Everyone can approve it because no one's saying anything.

But if you collectively agree to write definitive statements in clear language and big words then the process is very different. It takes longer. It involves more head-scratching hunts for exactly the right word and more arguments – because you're actually discussing what needs to be discussed. But that's how you get a tighter, brighter, lighter presentation.

Writing good means thinking good.

No Copy. No Paste. No Copy.
No Paste. No Copy. No Paste.
No Copy. No Paste. No Copy.
No Paste. No Copy. No Paste.
No Copy. No Paste. No Copy.
No Paste. No Copy. No Paste.
No Copy. No Paste. No Copy.
No Paste. No Copy. No Paste.
No Copy. No Paste. No Copy.
No Paste. No Copy. No Paste.
No Copy. No Paste. No Copy.

Practically, though...

Never copy and paste words into a presentation. That's how corporate/organisational buzzwords and jargon get in.

If you just select a paragraph of text from a report or email and paste it into your slide then that text feels like an unassailable, indivisible object. You feel less able to edit it and remove the jargon and the filler words.

It's much better to summarise it while you're writing your presentation.

Put it in your own words. That'll help stop the nonsense seeping in.

‘Big things are best said, are almost always said, in small words.’

Peggy Noonan

That will do

In 2005 the founders of YouTube needed to raise some money from venture capitalists to get their business going. If you google 'YouTube pitch deck' you can find their slides.

They are not a visual feast. They are just text, badly laid out, black-and-white, dull. Almost aggressively so. Right on the line between 'couldn't be bothered' and 'didn't need to bother'. But they are simple, clear and concrete. The first slide looks like this:

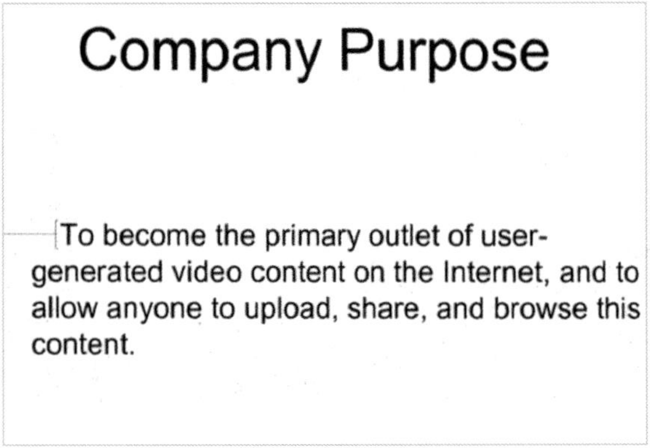
Company Purpose
To become the primary outlet of user-generated video content on the Internet, and to allow anyone to upload, share, and browse this content.

The rest of them follow in the same vein. The slides are stark, brutal and compelling.

Your first job is to match this level of simplicity, directness and clarity.

Get to here and you can stop if you want. You've done enough.

But, once you've got here, you can start to have fun. It's time for poetry and pictures.

Big pens, small spaces

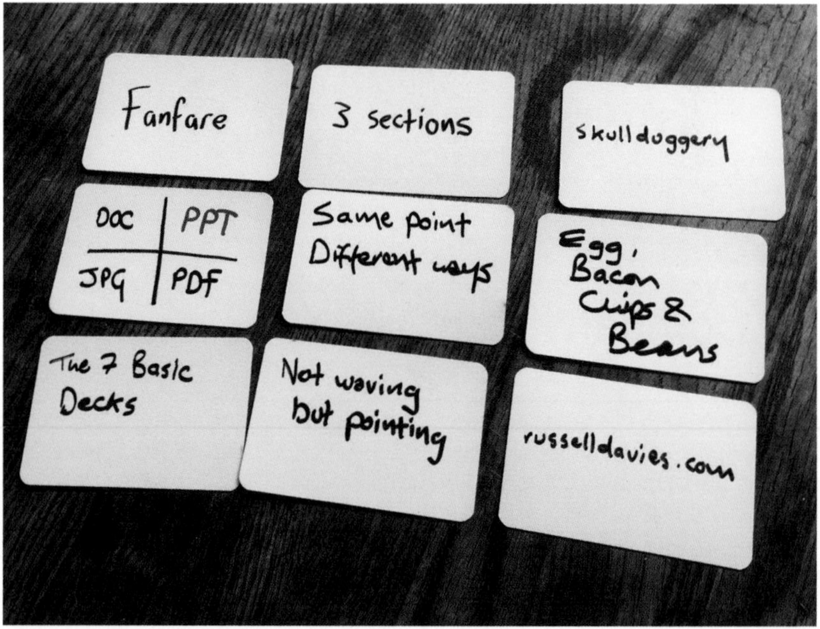

Practically, though…

It's very helpful when planning a presentation to step away from the screen.

A great way to start is with big pens and small cards. It gets you thinking in the right way from the beginning. It's impossible for you to write too much.

Personally, I find index cards too big so I use blank playing cards. They're just the right shape and size. You can buy vast quantities of them for not much money from a well-known online retailer.

Moleskine make a notebook designed for screenwriters/storyboarders that comes with a lot of little boxes on the page. Also perfect for this. It's how Hemingway used to write his PowerPoint.

If you read much about writing, you'll know there are two kinds of writer: 'plotters' and 'pantsers'. Plotters plan their story out at the beginning, before they start the actual writing. They know exactly what's going to happen, and when. Pantsers do it by the seat of their pants, i.e. they just start writing at page one and work it all out as they go.

The joy of PowerPoint is that you can do both. You're dealing with much less material than a TV script or a novel and it's easier to move around and alter. You can start and restart multiple times. Especially when you're still at the pen-and-paper stage. Go back and forth. Write some more cards. Move them around. It's fun.

You might find that the title for one of your three sections is wrong. Or that it's in the wrong order. But that's OK. You've only got three bits so it's not like your elaborately plotted edifice will suddenly collapse. Move some cards from column A to column B and you're done.

Three Short Words

SIMPLER
CLEARER
FASTER

Welcome to GOV.UK
The best place to find government services and information
Simpler, clearer, faster
Search on GOV.UK

Again with the threes

Threes don't just help structure your argument. They help you make it. They help you turn your recommendations into powerful, motivating, memorable language.

In rhetoric they're called tricolons.

For Kellogg's – Snap, Crackle, Pop.
For Dorothy Parker's choice in men – Handsome, Ruthless, Stupid.

Or there's a thing called a molossus – three short words. Yes We Can.
Out damned spot. DuckDuckGo.

Or there's epizeuxis: Location, location, location. Education, education, education.
Tora! Tora! Tora!

I once worked for the London Organising Committee of the Olympic Games, helping out with communications and strategy. Nothing I could write was as good or as simple as the official Olympic motto: Faster, Higher, Stronger.

When I went to work on GOV.UK, the government website, the product manager asked for a 'product vision' for what we were building. We wanted to make it easy to use, jargon-free and comprehensible, and stripped back and minimal so it would load blazingly fast. So I ripped off the Olympics and we wrote Simpler, Clearer, Faster.

A few years later I went to work with a renewable energy company. We had a deliberately straightforward product, competitive prices and lovely green tariffs. I was asked to write a slogan for the website. I wrote Simpler, Cheaper, Greener.

I'm not clever but I am consistent.

Stay home
Protect the NHS
Save lives

Why did everyone stumble over this?

During the early days of the pandemic I got obsessed with the way that politicians and pundits would stumble over the government's apparently excellent slogan 'Stay home. Protect the NHS. Save lives'. I eventually learned that it's because ears and brains have been trained (or are neurologically predisposed) to expect a list of three like this to come in a particular order.

Shortest items first, longest item last.

I came, I saw, I conquered. Crash, bang, wallop. Mad, bad and dangerous to know.

'Protect the NHS' should have been last.

This illustrates why three is such a powerful number in communication. Three is enough to establish a pattern and then either break it or confirm it. The ear is caught by something that goes short, short, long. The long is a little surprise.

On the *Rule Of Three* podcast they describe this pattern as set-up, confirm, confound.

That's perfect.

Write your threes like that. Short, short, long.

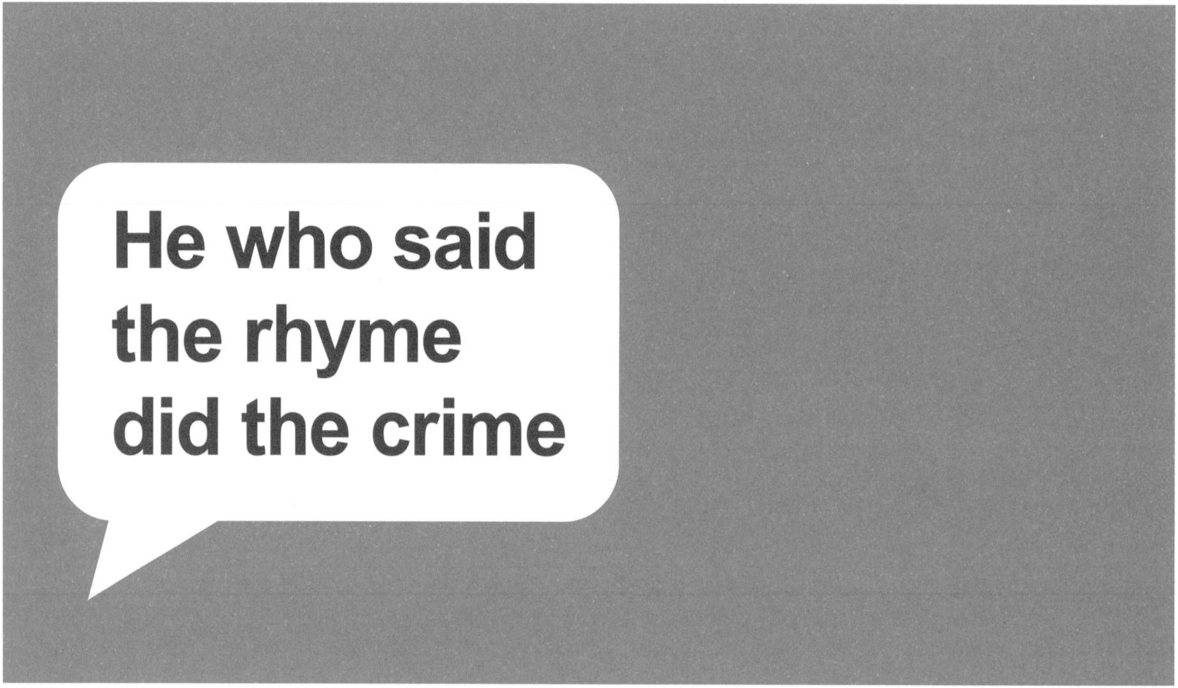
He who said the rhyme did the crime

If you've been the victim of a 1970s childhood in the UK you'll know that accusations of flatulence in the classroom or playground are often accompanied by the logical and rhetorical power of rhyme.*

This taps into something primal in the human psyche.

Things that rhyme just seem truer and more persuasive than things that don't.

It's known as the rhyme-as-reason effect or the Eaton-Rosen phenomenon.†

That's why you're advised that if you snooze you lose, or that you should fake it till you make it. It feels corny but it works.

If you want to know more I can recommend the fabulously titled paper 'Birds of a Feather Flock Conjointly (?): Rhyme as Reason in Aphorisms' (McGlone and Tofighbakhsh, 2000).

* This is part of the sequence employed in the East Midlands, *c.*1972–81. Wikipedia lists a comprehensive set of 'inculpatory pronouncements' in the Flatulence Humour section.

† Brilliantly, no one called Eaton or Rosen was ever involved in studying this. Apparently the names got accidentally appended to the Wikipedia article and then became so widely cited that it is, now, the actual name of the thing. This could only have been a better story if the name had rhymed. It sort of does, if you squint.

Leave it to Lee Longlands

I like a little alliteration

If you can't make things rhyme, or if it seems crass and forced, a great alternative is a little alliteration. It gets stuff stuck in our heads. As Mark Forsyth points out in *The Elements of Eloquence*, 'It takes two to tango, but it takes two to waltz as well.'

As he memorably puts it:

> Shakespeare simply knew that people are suckers for alliteration and that it's pretty damned easy to make something alliterate (or that it's surprisingly simple to add alliteration). You can spend all day trying to think of some universal truth to set down on paper, and some poets try that. Shakespeare knew that it's much easier to string together some words beginning with the same letter. It doesn't matter what it's about. It can be the exact depth in the sea to which a chap's corpse has sunk; hardly a matter of universal interest, but if you say, 'Full fathom five thy father lies', you will be considered the greatest poet who ever lived.

Lee Longlands is a historic family-owned furniture shop based in Birmingham. If you grew up in the Midlands in the 1970s and 1980s the phrase 'Leave it to Lee' will induce in you a positively Proustian rush of reminiscence. Accompanied by a cacophonous chorus of congas these words would be sung at you from their TV commercial:

> Leave it (leave it), leave it to Lee,
> leave it to Lee Longlands (Longlands)
> Leave it comfortably, elegantly, leave it
> Leave it (leave it), leave it to Lee,
> leave it to Lee Longlands (Longlands)
> Leave it tastefully, coordinately, playfully
> Leave it to Lee Longlands

I've just checked. I remember it word for word from forty years ago. That's the power of alliteration (and rhyme).

Bernadine Healy was an American cardiologist, the first female director of the US National Institutes of Health and an all-round superhuman persuader and communicator. And on her desk she had a sign that said this. Malcolm Gladwell's *Revisionist History* podcast will tell you all about her. Sign: author's own.

Shrink your sentences, beef up your verbs

These things sound dead simple, don't they? They are. But they're still effective.

Corporate sentences are often too long, shovelling a boatload of ideas into a long line of words, many of them polysyllabic. It feels like we're demonstrating our worth via vocabulary.

Don't do that.

Obvs.

Short sentences are clearer, quicker and easier to read.

But we also tend to pick weedy, noncommittal verbs. Vague verbs designed to conceal intention and responsibility. Picking more memorable ones helps to dodge that problem.

Personally, I've found that keeping 'strong verbs' in mind also helps me dance past the active/passive problem. I've read all the good advice about dumping the passive voice, about how it sounds mealy-mouthed and creepy. But I didn't do a lot of grammar at school and I'm never quite sure exactly what it is.

I do, however, remember that a verb is a 'doing word' and I can spot that 'dodge', 'dance' and 'resist' are all stronger verbs than 'avoid'.

US president Lyndon B. Johnson once asked his secretary of defence for a paper on the Vietnam War, something short and focused that he could remember. He said he wanted it to be 'four-letter words and short sentences'. Wise. Damn true.

You can only ~~select~~ pick

from the ~~thousand~~ ten hundred

most ~~popular~~ usual words.

Practically, though…

One final little tip for getting your language tight and sharp.

Type your text into the Up-Goer Five Text Editor (https://splasho.com/upgoer5/).

'Up Goer Five' is cartoonist Randall Munroe's explanation of how the Saturn V rocket works – using only the thousand most common words in the English language. (Or as he says, complying with his own rules, 'using only the ten hundred words people use the most often'.)

This will make you examine your word choice microscopically.

If you can write a presentation that's 'Up Goer compliant' you'll probably have thrown away jargon, nominalisations and acronyms.

It will have made you unpack dense compound words into their underlying commoner ones. You don't necessarily have to use the contortions it might force on you, but it will help you think again about your words and find some simpler ways through.

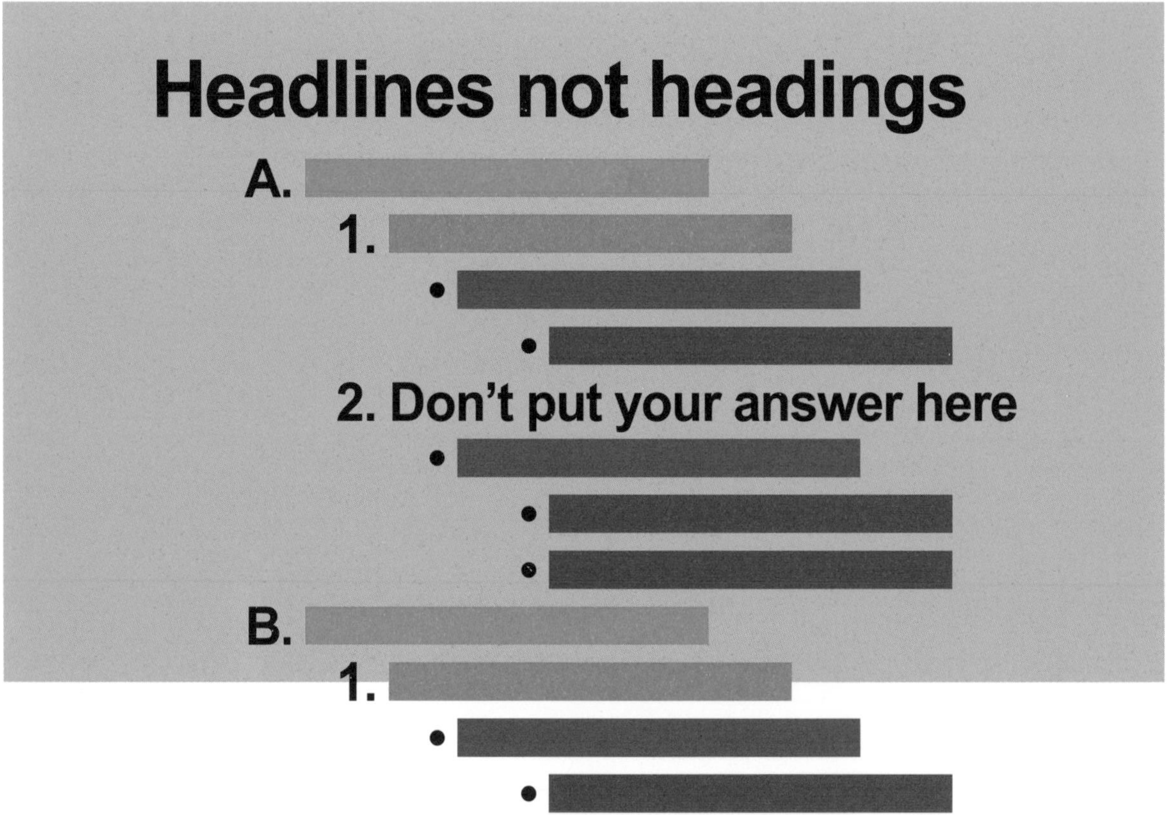
Headlines not headings
A.
1.
2. Don’t put your answer here
B.
1.

There's a bad PowerPoint habit you should try to abandon – writing headings.

People do it because the headings reflect how they're thinking about their presentation: 'I'm going to do a section on this, a section on that, and a section on the other.' And they write the section headings at the top of the slide and list all the information below it.

But that's not how people read. That's not how media works. That's not, for instance, how newspapers are written. The front page of a newspaper does not have a large heading that says 'Crime Update'. It has a headline that says 'Killer Strikes Again'.

Put the important information in the headline. Not in a subsequent bullet point.

Don't write a slide like this:

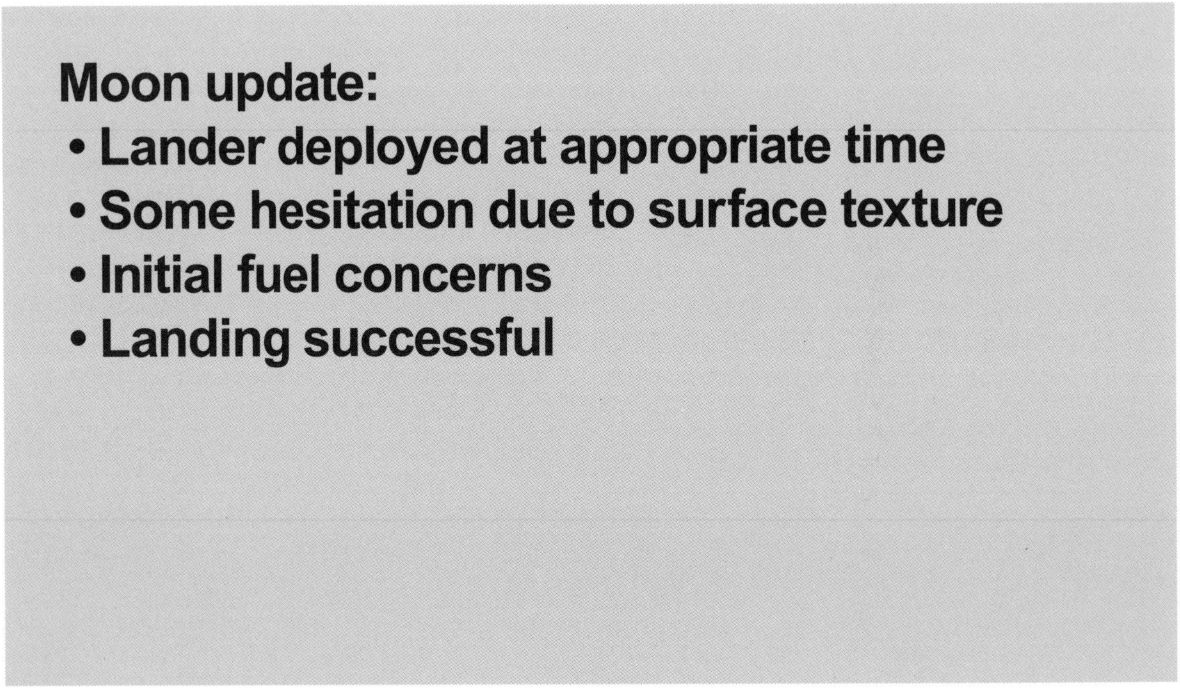

Moon update:
• Lander deployed at appropriate time
• Some hesitation due to surface texture
• Initial fuel concerns
• Landing successful

Do it like this:

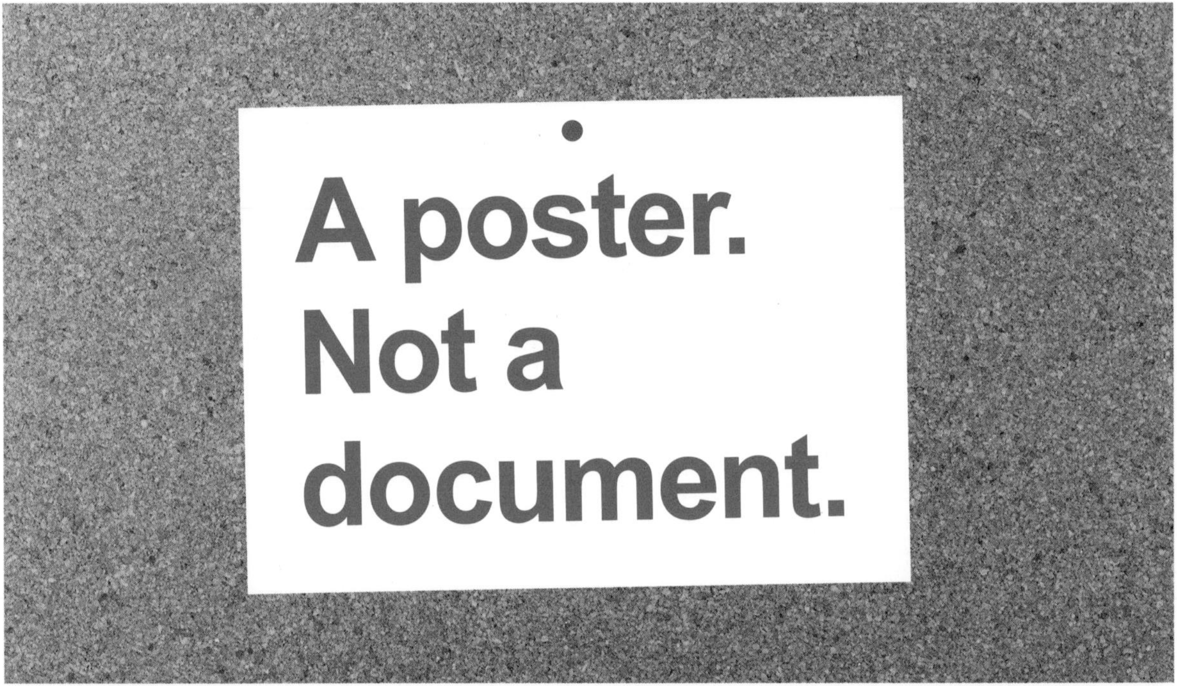
A poster.
Not a
document.

It helps to think of your presentation as a series of posters

One of the hardest ways to write a presentation is to begin at the beginning and just keep thinking logically and methodically what the next thing you should say is. That's what the logical brain might tell you to do but that's not the brain most humans are equipped with and that's not (mostly) how great bits of narrative art or persuasion are created. And, as we've discussed, it's not especially necessary with PowerPoint. One of the joys of the tool is the fact that putting things one after the other makes them seem connected. You don't need to worry about all the connective tissue that prose writers have to think about. In fact it's best if you don't think about prose at all. You should think of your presentation as a series of posters.

Each slide, while it's on screen, works almost exactly like a poster. It's got to be visually striking, memorable and arresting. It's got to have a point. It's got to make you want to do something.

A great way to write your deck is to start by working out what the two or three most striking and interesting things you're going to say are.

What would a poster for those things look like?

Would it be best in words or pictures or graphs or something else? Then make them as simple and direct as possible. Get them down to three or four words. Write them on Post-its and stare at them for a while. Draw them again. Try to lose a word. Live with them for a bit. Think about what you'll say when you stand in front of them. You're going to have two or three big moments when you do this presentation; the bits that people will remember and talk about. Make yourself an effective backdrop.

‘Nothing tastes as good as skinny feels.’

Kate Moss

Give the words a nudge

Kate Moss no longer stands by this reprehensible statement, but you've got to admit, she can turn a phrase. Short sentence, short words, strong verbs. Tick, tick, tick. All topped off with a discombobulating cognitive twist that turns it into something the brain itches to solve.

Shakespeare was particularly good at this, and scientists at the University of Liverpool reckon that's one reason we like him. They strapped electrodes to people's heads, got them to read Shakespeare, and discovered that:

> The brain reacts to reading a phrase such as 'he godded me' from the tragedy of *Coriolanus*, in a similar way to putting a jigsaw puzzle together. If it is easy to see which pieces slot together you become bored of the game, but if the pieces don't appear to fit, when we know they should, the brain becomes excited. By throwing odd words into seemingly normal sentences, Shakespeare surprises the brain and catches it off guard in a manner that produces a sudden burst of activity – a sense of drama created out of the simplest of things.*

Shakespeare or supermodel? You decide.

> I never did a dirty armpit.
> You can look dirty, but you can't be dirty.
>
> Go prick thy face.
>
> It's a sin to be tired.
>
> We might have met them dareful.
>
> Years and years of crying. Oh, the tears!
>
> But, bear-like, I must fight the course.
>
> You can't do a dog in a heel.
>
> We might all burst into flames.
>
> If I do a midcalf look, I look bandy.

(Head to www.russelldavies.com/powerpoint for the answers.)

* This is exactly what I want scientists to be doing all day. Well done, boffins, textbook stuff.

A poster
with a
poem on it

Or you could think of it as poetry

You can learn a lot from poets and the way they play with words and compress meaning into tiny packages.

This is my favourite. It's by Andrew Michael Roberts.

> the moon
>
> all the other moons
> get their own names

It's tiny yet twisty. Regular words. Big idea. I'd love to sit through a presentation that worked like that.

It also leaves room for the mouse.

There was a legendary San Francisco adman in the 1960s called Howard Gossage. He was like a character from *Mad Men* except real and not a complete arse. When talking about writing ads he liked to say, 'When baiting a trap with cheese, always remember to leave room for the mouse.' By which he meant, when you're constructing a persuasive story make sure you don't have so much clarity and detail that there's no thinking left for your audience to do.

Five reasons you should use lists:

1. They wake people up. Honestly.
2. Put a list on the screen and people will stir in their seats, sit up a bit, get out their phones and their notebooks and start writing it down.
3. People love lists.
4. They seem valuable, like repositories of knowledge. Like you're finally going to stop messing around and deliver some actual knowledge.
5. They're easy to write.

Seven more reasons you should use lists:

1. They're a good discipline; they make you organise your thoughts into a useful format.
2. They're a great, simple way of structuring a talk.
3. Five Reasons We Should Do X is a perfectly acceptable format for a presentation.
4. You can still do jokes.
5. Just by messing around with the form.
6. See.
7. Bang.

Eleven more compelling list facts:

1. They're clear. We know what we're getting.
2. We remember things spatially – lists are memorable because we can remember that was the top one and this is the second one.
3. That's why we have shopping lists on long bits of paper and not on wide ones.
4. As A. S. Byatt put it, 'lists are a form of power'. They put you in control.
5. We know where we are. This is the fifth one. We know we're almost halfway.
6. They're a scannable, easy-to-pay-attention-to way to absorb information.
7. Don't put too many on one slide though – spread them over a few.
8. And don't reveal them all at once – people will read ahead.
9. Prime numbers are more memorable. A Top 11 is more interesting than a Top 10.
10. They provide all sorts of ways to make things more interesting. Like tell people that one of the items on the list isn't true and get them to work out which one. That keeps people watching.
11. They feel definitive and completable. Look! This is the last one. We're done. We can all go home now.

Design is easy

Everything communicates

A friend of a friend of mine, a communications strategist who used to find all talk of design and fonts very tedious, once had a revelation and summed it up perfectly:

> Strategy is like food – how it looks matters.

Whatever you're presenting, whether it's a strategy, a budget recommendation or your theories about Why Dora Is the Worse Explora, the look of your slides is as important to how it's consumed as the redness of wine or the pinkness of shrimp.

This does not mean it's difficult. It's not – it's easy. There are just a few things to think about.

The first one is this: your first duty is to make your slides accessible to everyone in the room. That starts with making them readable.

Don't make your slides so intricate and clever that people can't read them. Do not design for seventeen-year-olds with perfect eyesight sitting right next to the screen. Think about regular people who might have eyesight problems and might be sitting at the back.

Dead big type. Never have more than three bullet points per slide and never have more than six words per line. Start with that.

#NOTALLCAPS

Practically, though…

Even at that size, there will be people in your audience who will have trouble seeing or reading your slides. They might have sight or cognitive difficulties. Or they might have trouble hearing what you say. They might not have your language as their first language.

If you design your slides with them in mind you'll make things better for everyone.

There are great guides to the specifics of doing this well online, but here are the basics.

Words: at least 30pt, a familiar sans serif font, only one font per slide. Avoid too much underlining or too many italics. Left-aligned text. This will help people with sight problems as well as people with dyslexia. Include lots of white space. Do not use ALL CAPS. It's very tempting because it makes the words look neater – they're all the same height. But that also makes them harder to read.

Colour: high contrast; don't have a white background – it gets very glary. If you want a light background use grey. But the best combination is a dark-blue background and white text. And don't use colour as the only way to convey information.

Charts: as simple as you can; only include the information you need to make your point.

Video/audio: make sure it's captioned.

Notes/handouts: having handouts is always a good idea. Make them available beforehand. Make them properly accessible. Again, there are guides to doing this well all over the internet.

Make it big and readable and your presentation will be better than most. If your words are clear and memorable you're going to do well.

The next level is to exploit PowerPoint's special powers. You can combine words, typography and imagery.

Authoritative

Playful

Paula Scher is one of the world's leading graphic designers. Her designs make type come alive with meaning. She said this and she makes it happen:

> Words have meaning and typography has feeling. When you put them together it's a spectacular combination.

PowerPoint lets you make a billion different type choices. Some will undermine your meaning and some will support it. Some fonts look authoritative and some look playful. The joy of PowerPoint is you can try out different ones and see how they look. Please do this. Experiment. Have fun. This is why doing PowerPoint is better than doing expenses.

But only do it for as long as it's fun. If it starts getting stressy and making you anxious then stop and choose one of the six or seven basic fonts. You are not Paula Scher. Please don't feel you have to be.

Stefanie Posavec (who designed this book) says the open-source sans serif fonts found on Google Fonts are a good bet, as many were designed by some of the best typeface designers working today. She's a fan of 'Inter', which you can find there.

And if you're worried about your presentation not working on someone else's computer, it's safest to use one of the 'system fonts' - the ones that actually come with the machine.

Don't
Emphasise
Everything

It's easy to get carried away with emphasis. You want to make a point. You want to be clear and focused about which *point you're making*. It's **important**. You want to *emphasise* the **important** bits.

But this makes everything hard to read and you look like you're not sure what point you're making.

If you've kept your words short and clear you shouldn't need much emphasis.

If you feel like underlining things, it's a good clue that you need to rewrite them.

Stick to one form of emphasis per presentation. And use it sparingly.

Your first duty is to choose a set of colours that will make your presentation readable and accessible. Choose contrasting colours. Don't have pink on a pink background. Remember that lots of people are colourblind.

If you'd like to you can spend absolutely ages playing around with colours. It's fun. The colours you choose will make some sort of statement about your content.

But do this first...

When we were creating GOV.UK we were lucky enough to work with legendary designer Margaret Calvert. She was co-designer of the system of road signs developed in the UK in the 1950s, used to this day and influential around the world. She was obsessed with readability and knew a lot about it. We wanted her guidance on how to make the website as clear and easy to read as possible.

She told us to design everything in black-and-white first. Get it to work like that, and only add colour once everything was clear and readable in monotones. That is brilliant advice for PowerPoint. Start like that.

And these days, if you do your slides in simple black-and-white, maybe with just a single, stark accent colour like a bright red, or with a red and a green to make your data clearer, you will stand out at any conference.

And then you can start to think about imagery. This is where the fun starts and PowerPoint begins to show what it can do – make words and pictures work together.

Remember, though, that you're designing posters and a good poster is always simple. The point of imagery is not to make your slides look more whizzy or fancy. The point is to make your point.

Use images to add something extra, not just to make the slides look pretty.

Don't use clip art. Clip art, almost by definition, is the visual embodiment of a cliché.

It's a dead metaphor.

If you're talking about money and budgets and funding you don't need pictures of money, even if you're in the finance department.

Everyone knows what money looks like.

Personally, though, I love a big red cross through things. Very effective.

Practically, though...

You should watch the films of Mira Nair (*Monsoon Wedding, A Suitable Boy*). You'll be struck by the use of colour. The colours help tell the story and create a unified aesthetic. Nair does this by creating lookbooks for each film – scrapbooks, shared with her production teams, that everyone can use for a reference. It's a crucial part of her creative process.

If the black/white/red example is too stark for you this is another way to think about the aesthetics and design of your slides. Make yourself a lookbook.

Consider your subject, the stuff you're going to be talking about and the points you want to make. Study the aesthetics of it. Collect examples. Look at the fonts, the colours, the type of images. Then work out what will help you communicate. Do you want to fit into that world or stand out from it? Do the same or do the opposite? What's the mood going to be? Getting gradually more optimistic? Punctuated by big moments? Loud, quiet, loud? You can do that with colour.

The writer and critic Susan Sontag once said that 'every style is a means of insisting on something'. The look of your slides can be part of your insistence.

The slides on the next page, for instance, are from Rachel Coldicutt's presentation: Can We Occupy Technology With Love? They're designed to evoke the late-1990s internet community GeoCities because Rachel was making a point about the value of things that don't look that valuable:

> Perhaps the innovations that are sold with good PowerPoints and slick pitches are only really more important than sea shanties on TikTok because they are dressed up to look more important.

SATURDAY 2ND MAY
9:30pm BST
SHARED
GOOGLE
DOC
PARTY
(it's a party in a Shared
google doc)
DRESS CODE:
ANONYMOUS ANIMALS
Party in a Shared Google Doc
What if no one comes?

Data
algorithms
gig workers

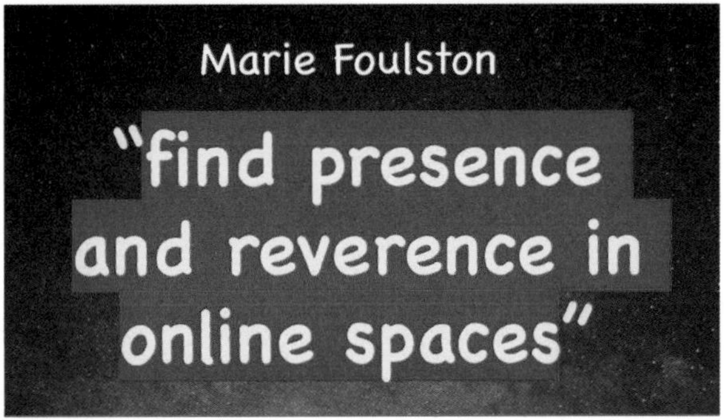
Marie Foulston
"find presence and reverence in online spaces"

And pay a little attention to how it feels

Look at the shapes on the right. If you were asked to decide which shape is called 'bouba' and which is called 'kiki', what would you say? You'd say 'bouba' is on the bottom, right? Most people do. There's a connection between how things look, how they sound and what they end up meaning. When you're thinking about your design take a step back every now and then and make sure the overall vibe of the thing is consonant with what you're trying to communicate.

Are you trying to be optimistic? Do your slides feel that way? Are you trying to get everyone focused on some numbers? Does your design feel numerate?

Your unconscious is good at this stuff – if your design feels off it might need a nudge. Maybe tweak a font or warm up the colours, but don't worry about it too much.

Is it readable? Then you're fine.

The world is full of slides

When you're out in the world, just keep your eyes open. There are messages and ideas all around you. Collect them. Take a photo and one day it'll be handy for a presentation.

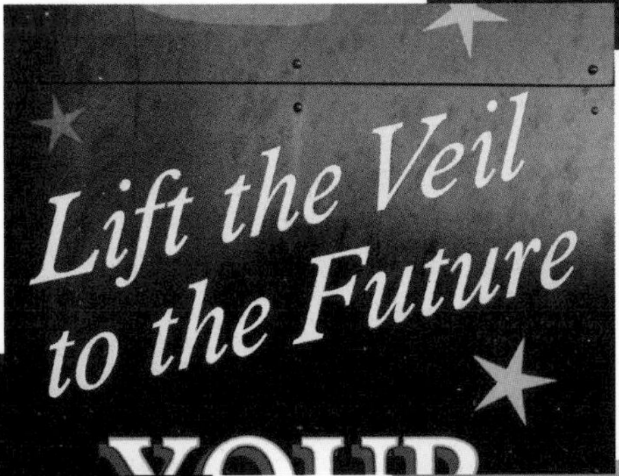

I'm going to say it again: palimpsest. There's nowt as palimpsesty as PowerPoint and this is a magnificent example. It's like a 'you are here' for the brain. The choice of a default font and basic arrows is part of the statement. They're flung onto the graph like feminist graffiti on a Fiat poster. Angry but not surprised.

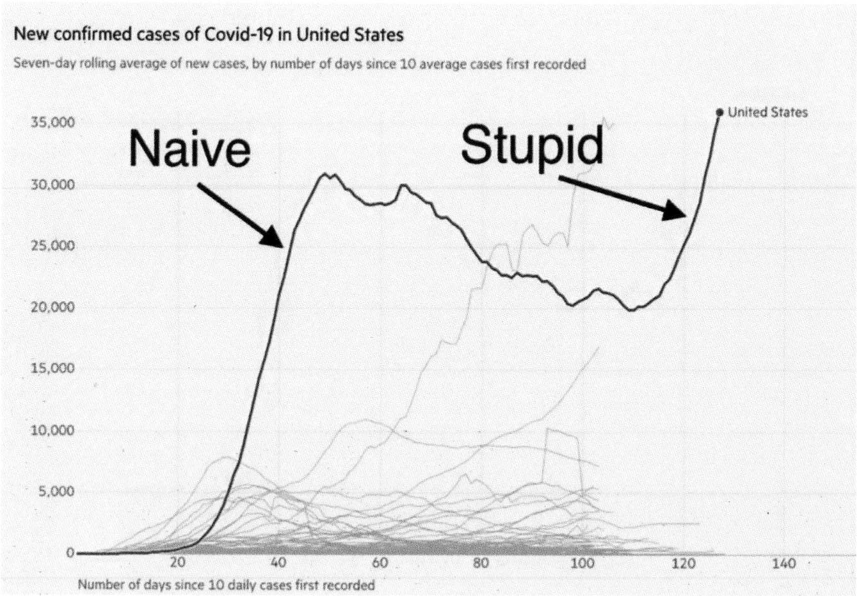

You can't be too obvious

Getting a message out of one brain and into another is a miracle.

Your idea (stored in some poorly understood biochemical reactions in your brain, a lump of offal floating in a box of bone) has to be translated through more chemicals and nerves into physical motion of fleshy lumps like eyes or hands and then into waves of air, marks on a surface like paper or electromechanical impulses on a computer. Then there's more transference via air, electricity, biochemistry and physics. And, if PowerPoint's involved, a considerable degree of software licensing. Then there's the complicated business of the ears, eyes and sensibilities of the recipient before you get the thing through their bonebox and into their fleshy lump.

No wonder you sometimes have to repeat things.

Which is why I love it when people do data design like this. It's generous. It shows people where to look.

This is a tweet from an epidemiologist called Owais Raza (@reye27). He's taken coronavirus data and made us look at it again – and understand it. It's a layer of clear, opinionated storytelling on top of a wall of data.

If you can't bring yourself to scribble on your pristine graphs then this is how you should talk about them when you do your presentation. Point at the relevant bits, explain what they mean. Show the data and tell people what you think about it.

Give them enough understanding that they can decide if they agree with you.

Word
clouds
Disappointing
Unnecessary
Cloudy
Empty
Inconsequential
Baffling
Useless
Wordcloud
Unproductive
Absurd
Silly
Aimless
Ineffective
Irritating
Irrelevant
Redundant
Flashy

Gimmicky
Futile
Unhelpful
Cloud
Daft
Annoying
Pointless
Grim
Vague
Fruitless
don't
Senseless
Meaningless
Unclear
Indistinct
Stupid
Lazy
Forbidding
help
Valueless

Fabiola Gianotti is an experimental particle physicist who led one of the two CERN teams whose work resulted in the discovery of the Higgs boson. She was nominated to be *Time* magazine's Person of the Year 2012. But her fame is also, now irretrievably, linked to her decision to announce the 'God particle' using Comic Sans. As she told *Symmetry* magazine, she did so 'because I like it. It's so cute ... I find it a sweet and pleasant font.' She's right. And perhaps the innocence and naivety of Comic Sans is exactly the right way to speak of momentous things. It beckons us in. It's inclusive. Don't worry, says Comic Sans, all are welcome here. We're just not at home to type snobs.

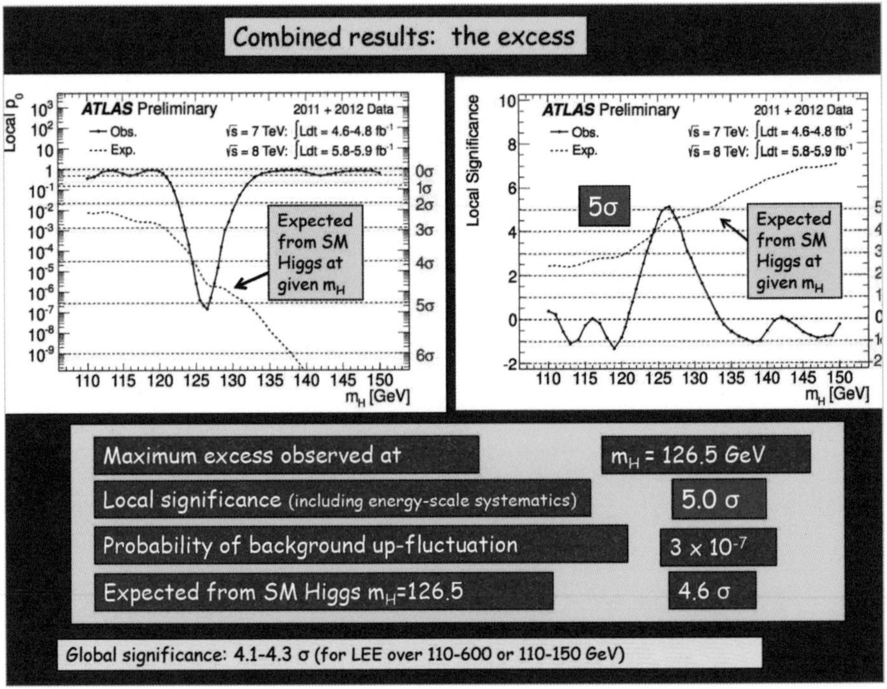

Don't be too general public-y

This is the slide that told the world the Higgs Boson had been found. The actual discovery of the 'God particle' got only slightly more news coverage than the fact that the scientist responsible had used Comic Sans to announce it. Designers threw up their mouse pads in horror.

But to many (especially fellow scientists) what this slide crime signalled was Real Science. This person clearly didn't care about graphic design, PR, marketing or spin.* This was someone who just cared about the science.

Kate Moran is a User Experience researcher. In 2017 she wrote up her work looking at what scientists and researchers find credible about data.

One of her respondents described a nice-looking website like this:

> This one looked a little more … general public-y. It has this nice big picture that fills the whole screen, I've noticed that recently with websites. It looks nice, it looks great. But that tells me someone's putting a lot of effort into making it look great.

And when shown something less polished they said:

> I'm looking at the real thing. Not an artist's conception of what the real thing is. This looks like it was made by a geeky scientist … It looks like real data, not massaged.

I've heard something similar from entrepreneurs and start-up people. They're suspicious if you've spent too much time polishing your slides. Remember, you're trying to look like an expert in whateveritisthatyoudo, not an expert in PowerPoint.

* Not that kind of spin, anyway. They obviously cared about the amount of angular momentum associated with a subatomic particle or nucleus and measured in multiples of the Dirac h, or h-bar (ħ), equal to the Planck constant divided by 2π.

Genchi Genbutsu

Practically, though…

> You can't come up with a good story idea in the office. I've never had a good idea that I just came up with out of thin air. It always comes from being on the ground.
>
> Hannah Dreier, reporter at the *Washington Post* and winner of the 2019 Pulitzer Prize for Feature Writing (i.e. someone who knows about this stuff)

One of the simplest ways to make a presentation better is take some pictures of the thing you're talking about. And take them yourself. Don't just google them.

Too many presentations are too abstract. They're full of diagrams and representations and metaphors. There's no substitute for the actual experience of going somewhere, having a look and documenting the experience.

Going there will also help you understand the problem better. That'll lead to a better explanation and it might lead to a better solution. The legendary Toyota Production System (the process that has transformed the manufacturing of almost everything in the last fifty years) has a phrase for this: *Genchi Genbutsu* (roughly, 'go to where the problem is').

Then make it concrete

You've got three main sections to your presentation. Make sure there's something concrete in each. We remember concrete things, not abstractions. People, objects, places. Or things happening to people, objects or places.

For example:

Jon Steel is a legend of advertising strategy. That means he spends a lot of time thinking about how to communicate on behalf of his clients, a lot of time researching how real people think about communications and a lot of time doing incredibly important presentations that could result in huge wins for his advertising agency. He's very good at all those things and he's written a very good book about it called *Perfect Pitch*.

In it he describes his agency's pitch for the Porsche account. Porsche weren't doing well in the US at the time. He needed to find a way to get across to the Porsche people that lots of people hated them. This is a surprisingly difficult thing to tell a large corporation. You'd imagine that hard-nosed business people were, in fact, hard-nosed but no, they hate you telling them that everyone thinks they suck. I used to work with Microsoft. I know.

So Jon did a clever thing. He used a drawing from some focus groups they'd done. He'd given these drawings to non-Porsche drivers and asked them to write in the speech bubble what they'd be thinking in the circumstances.

This single image crystallised the whole multimillion-dollar problem for Porsche in the US. And Jon's agency won the pitch.

This wasn't just a lucky accident. Jon knows what he's doing. If you have to deliver bad news, being able to point to the screen and say, 'It's not me saying it, it's them,' is both more credible and more comfortable. Jon is also very smart in his commissioning of research. He was looking for insights about how people felt about Porsche but he was also looking for evidence and concrete artefacts he could use in the final presentation. Clever.

ASSHOLE!
YOU
PORSCHE

HEY
LOOK

If you're still a little apprehensive about the look of your slides, here are two other ways to think about it, inspired by a wonderful blog post by Austin Kleon called 'Pointing At Things'.

Hedda Sterne described the purpose of art as saying, 'Hey, look!'

> The intention, the purpose, is not to show your talent but to show something … I had a very great urgency to show, to share. The cat brings you in things, you know? It was that kind of thing. I discovered things and wanted to share them.

If you're putting visuals in your deck you should think of it as saying, 'Hey, look! I've got something to show you. Here it is.'

Make things bigger

And the wonderful artist Sister Corita Kent denied that she made art. She said:

> I just make things I like bigger, assuming that if I like them some other people might too.

You could also think of your visuals like that. Just find things you like and make them bigger. Way bigger. That'll make for a great presentation.

If your presentation is you finding things you think are interesting, making them bigger and pointing at them, you'll do a great job.

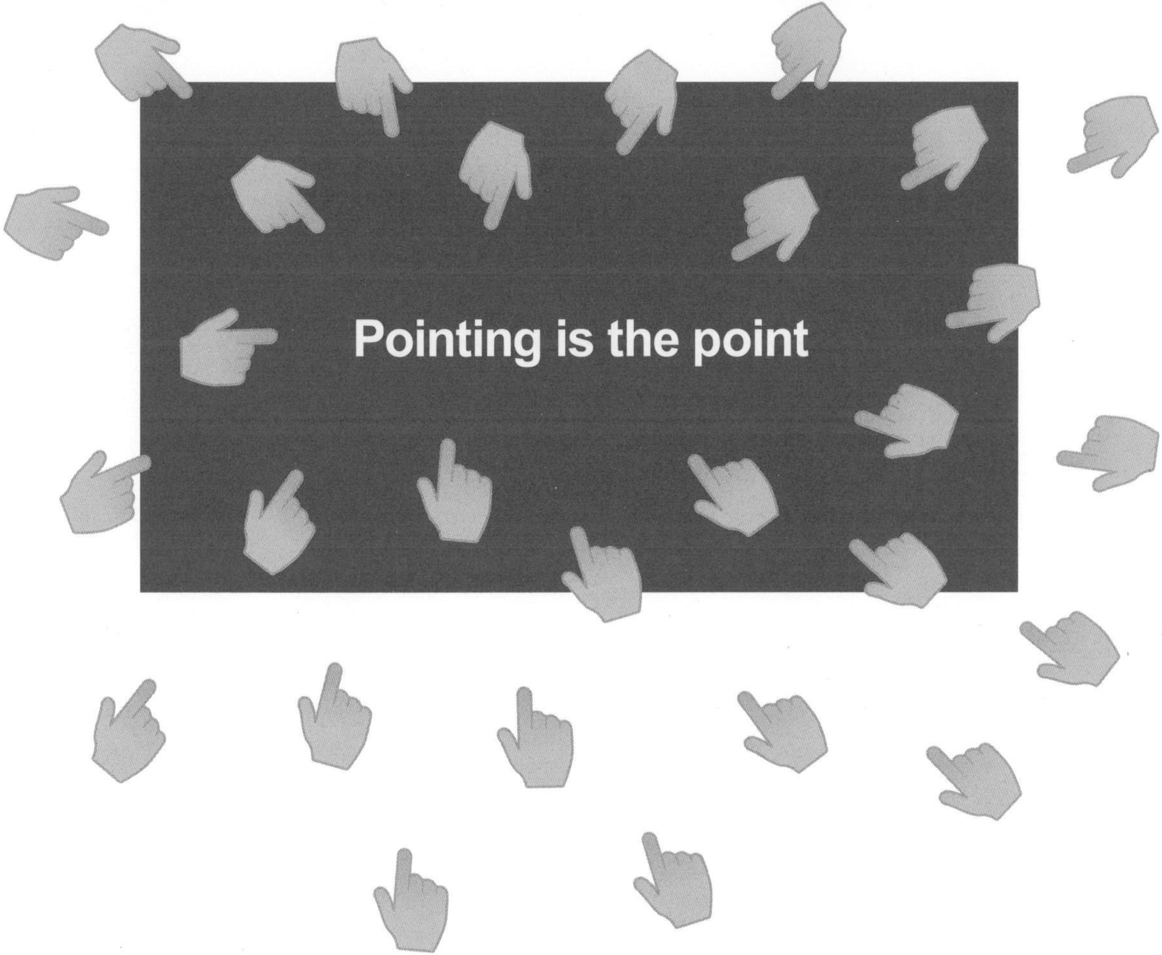
Pointing is the point

And then you just have to present it

Before we go any further, let's talk about the elephant in the conference centre.

There are a lot of books about presenting whose advice boils down to: have tons of charisma, like Steve Jobs. This is not good advice. The German sociologist Max Weber first advanced the notion of charismatic leadership and described it as a

> …certain quality of an individual personality, by virtue of which he is set apart from ordinary men and treated as endowed with supernatural, superhuman, or at least specifically exceptional powers or qualities.

The point, the joy, the success of PowerPoint is that you don't need to be superhuman to be good at it. It's for everyone.

Again – you don't have to be Steve Jobs. But there are some things you can learn from him.

First, he prepared and practised a lot. A real lot. More than you're imagining. He would start working on a presentation about three months before doing it. Hours a day. Every day. He would share early versions with loads of different people for critique and improvement (a technique he learned from Pixar). He would never write a script, but would spend time getting his slides in the right order and then rehearsing, rehearsing and rehearsing until he knew exactly what he was going to say but could do so in a natural, spontaneous-seeming way.

Second, Jobs always used striking language and compelling comparisons. When he launched the iPhone 3G he described it as 'amazingly zippy'. Not many tech company leaders would have the guts or imagination to boil their incredible technological achievement down to something a twelve-year-old might say. But that made it all the more striking and memorable.

Jobs was a great presenter. He was at home on a stage. He had charisma. But you don't have to be like him. His secret was being a bigger version of himself. You can do that.

It's not like in the films or on TV

You've probably experienced the Gell-Mann Amnesia effect.

You're watching the news and they start talking about something you know well. Your work, hobby or special interest. You realise they're getting it horribly and massively wrong. They're generalising unhelpfully and some details are just plain incorrect. You're horrified and appalled. Journalists know nothing! And then they move on to the next item, about banking or unemployment or whatever and you assume that, in every other instance, they're broadly getting it right.

I always think of the Gell-Mann Amnesia effect when I see presentations in films or on TV. They're always very, very unlike presentations in real life.

Screenwriters treat presentations like closing arguments in courtrooms, or calls to arms before battle. They love them. As do actors. It's when they get to show off. It's an opportunity for a speech, a soliloquy. Important things will be decided through powerful language and a high-voltage exchange of ideas.

Do not be misled by this. It's not what you're aiming for and real-life presentations are not like that. No one says, 'Goddamit! I'm going to give you the whole of GlobeStar's worldwide advertising account right now!' when you've finished your slides.

There are merely some desultory questions and a promise to get back to you soon.

That's OK. That's good. You did good.

> **'People pay to see others believe in themselves.'**
>
> **Kim Gordon**

This is, after all, the point of the whole thing. You're creating something that benefits from your presence, from you being in the room, from your interaction with the slides and the audience.

If you're not adding anything then you should just send the slides in advance and everyone can read them.

But this doesn't mean you have to become a superhuman performer. You don't. You just have to be there and be yourself. As the choreographer Martha Graham has it: 'The body says what words cannot.' You being there, being you, exuding youness, is powerful.

And it doesn't have to be *exactly* you. You probably have an Instagram you. The you with a little more polish, whose knick-knacks are a little more elegantly arranged. Do that, but for PowerPoint. Summon up a PowerPoint persona who's the same you but with a little more energy and oomph. Swing your arms round your head for thirty seconds before you start, to get your energy up. Be slightly louder and brighter than you ordinarily would. That's all you need.

Joanne McNeil says this in her magnificent book *Lurking*:

> A sociologist once told me that before the internet, *The Presentation of Self in Everyday Life* by Erving Goffman was a difficult text to teach. Now students get it. They perform a self in one app or website, while other aspects of their identity are on full blast in different internet channels.

Maybe that's why 'kids these days' are so good at PowerPoint. They're very used to this idea.

‘If you’re not nervous, you’re not paying attention.’

Miles Davis

PowerPoint is here to help

Everyone gets nervous, that's inevitable. A presentation is an important moment. You're occupying people's time and attention. That's bound to create some heightened feelings. The trick is to let your nerves push you into doing the right thing.

If you know your material well, if you've been through the slides dozens of times, if you've practised the presentation in front of friends, if you're confident about your opening and close (and if they're ones you've done before), if you're just going to be yourself … you're going to be a lot less nervous.

Lean into the PowerPoint. Let it help you. If there are words you think you'll struggle to say, put them on the slides. If you think you're going to forget stuff, put it in the notes.

Remember, don't think of it as a speech. It's not a speech. You're not trying to improvise a rousing pep talk before your team goes out and secures an underdog victory. You're describing a series of slides.

Imagine you were showing a group of friends some stuff you'd made or collected. Your Roman coins. Your knitted owls. Your prime ministerial Toby Jugs. You'd hold each one up, you'd tell them something interesting, you'd move on to the next one. Perhaps you'd do it in some meaningful order. Chronologically. By size. By the extent to which they did that annoying pointing thing with their thumbs.

If you do it right, that's all a presentation is. You talking to people about some slides you've made or collected. These are things you know a lot about.

You'll be fine.

It's ~~fine~~
~~all right~~
OK to ~~scream~~
~~rage~~
howl at the ~~stars~~
~~sky~~
moon

As I was writing this page my friend Rachel tweeted:

> When people write those 'this is how to write talks' guides, they never include the bit where you lie on the floor and howl at the moon and say, 'I hate myself why did I agree to do this?! I have no thoughts! What is wrong?!' And if they did no one would probably ever do talks.

She's right. Let's remember that part of the fun of a presentation is that you're doing something daring and unusual. You're doing something creative. You have to come up with ideas. Or at least marshal ideas into an interesting order. You have to do some phrase-making and some design. These are, for many people, unfamiliar things to do. That's why they're worth doing – but give yourself a break for finding them difficult.

PowerPoint can help you but sometimes there will be some howling at the moon.

That's why the next page is so important.

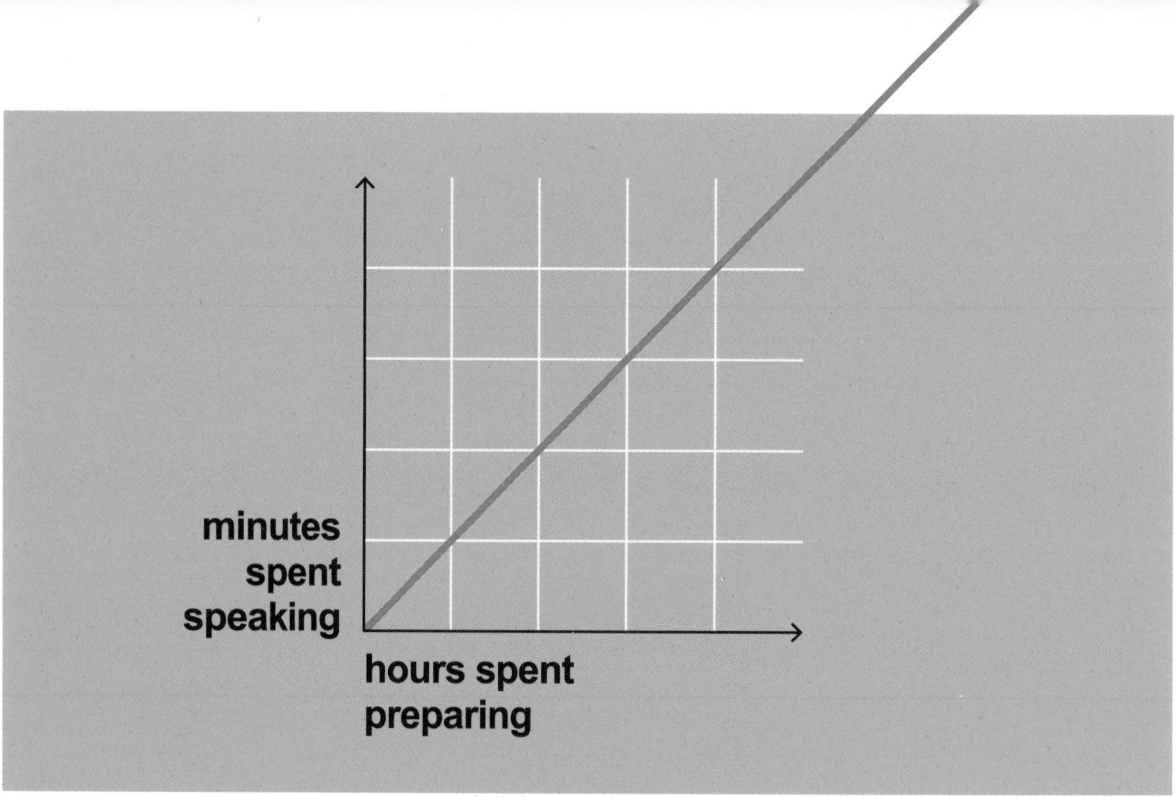
minutes spent speaking
hours spent preparing

Spend one hour preparing for every minute you'll be presenting

This is the big secret. Spend A LOT of time preparing and rehearsing. We've seen how much time Steve Jobs spent. Think about other performers. Comedians will spend months and years honing their act.

There's a magnificent interview with the magician Teller of Penn & Teller in *Esquire* magazine. He talks about the extraordinary amount of time it takes to make a magic trick work. Multiple hours a day for multiple months and years. As he puts it: 'Sometimes magic is just someone spending more time on something than anyone else might reasonably expect.' That's often the secret of a great presentation.

What you're seeing as charisma, genius or magic is just practice.

That's why I suggest one hour per minute as a useful rule of thumb.

I know that's a huge amount of time. It will sound impossible to a lot of you. This is why reusing material is so helpful.

But putting in that time gives you real confidence and security – enough confidence to improvise. And the confidence to improvise makes presenting fun. As Shannon Mattern tweeted:

> It's sometimes nice to be reminded that your most unprepared, extemporaneous performances can be the most organic and comfortable. You remember: oh, wow, I actually *know* this stuff in my bones.

Prep is a diversity issue

And here's something else to think about, especially if you're someone's boss.

If you want the presentations in your organisation to be good (and you should), then you need to carve out the time for people to prepare. Presentations are often requested at the last minute. They're often devalued as work. And organisations – and bosses – tend to assume that people will write their presentations 'around' their normal work. This time is often harder for women to find than men. They tend to be busier in the office and have less 'spare' time at home.

(Ella Fitzsimmons has written more about this at https://www.doingpresentations.com/prepare-diversity.html. It's good. You should read it.)

Find out if you are a violin or a cello

The writer Lucy Prebble once talked on a podcast about writing for different actors, about trying to find the right voice for them. She said, 'Some actors are violins, some actors are cellos.'

And with practice and enough performances that's what you'll discover. You don't have to try to be anything. You don't have to make yourself into something you're not. But do this a few times and you'll start to know more about 'your instrument' and what suits you. Then it'll get even easier. Do it for a few years and you'll be a natural. As Miles Davis once said: 'It takes a long time to sound like yourself.'

Practise early, practise often

When you're preparing a presentation practising is editing and editing is practising. Your finished product is not your deck, it's you presenting it. It's the slides plus the performance. So your editing process needs to acknowledge that – you need to make sure that the totality communicates, not just that you've spellchecked your document.

This isn't just about eliminating mistakes. Editing and rehearsal will help you work out what you want to say. Stephen King says that he often doesn't know what a book is about until he gets to the second draft. Emma Coats of Pixar will tell you the same thing:

> Trying for theme is important, but you won't see what the story is actually about till you're at the end of it. Now rewrite.

You don't have to know everything before you start. The writing is part of the process.

As the *New Yorker* journalist Kathryn Schulz says:

> The engine of writing is almost always ignorance. I write to figure out what I think.

So, early on in the process, when you think you've got your big finish and your three main points sorted out, go and find someone who doesn't know anything about the topic and just talk it through with them. Tell them the story, see what they think. They might say something useful.

More importantly, you'll find out what you think.

Do that again when you've got your first slides. Show them to someone and talk them through. You'll realise you've got them in the wrong order.

And do it again when you think you're finished. And then...

‘Where you falter, alter.’

Peggy Noonan

Rehearsal is composition

Peggy Noonan there folks – genius.

She wrote speeches for some reprehensible human beings but she sure could sling words.

Peggy's (rhyming!) advice here is perfect. Go through your presentation. Say what you're planning to say and if you stumble or forget a bit, change it. And, now you think about it, maybe the point you want to make is subtly different. It's slightly something else.

PowerPoint is like theatre. You should 'workshop' your presentation like actors and a director will workshop a play or a film. Read it through, try different approaches, change the words, change the scenes, cut a scene.

Do it in front of people you trust. Colleagues, friends, whoever. Listen to what they say. Change things.

Zadie Smith once wrote: 'Talking to yourself can be useful. And writing means being overheard.'

Writing and rehearsing a presentation is another version of this. Hearing yourself say what you think helps you make more sense of it.

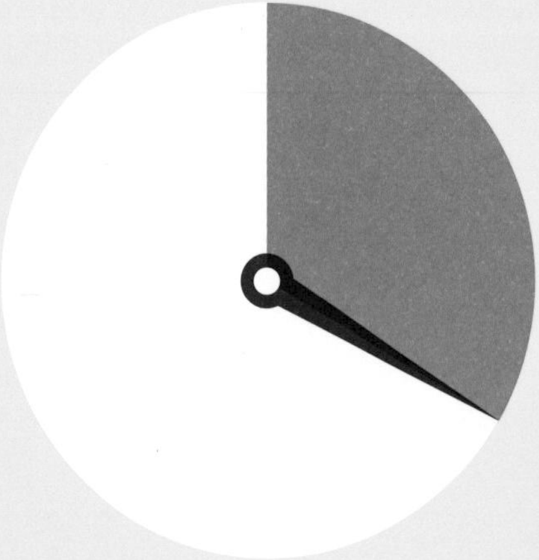

Only talk for twenty minutes

Bill Clinton is a gifted public speaker but even he can't fight physics. And it's simple human physics* that people find it difficult to pay attention for very long. His first major appearance on a national stage was at the Democratic Party Convention in 1988. He was supposed to talk for fifteen minutes but he dragged it out to thirty-three. He was getting boos and jeers until eventually he said, 'In conclusion,' and was greeted with loud, ironic cheers.

Pundits at the time speculated this was going to kill his political career.

Comedians have learned the same thing: attention flags after twenty minutes and then again at forty minutes.

So think hard if someone asks you to talk for longer than twenty minutes. Sustaining people's attention for any longer than that is very hard to do.

Peggy Noonan had particularly cogent advice on this matter: 'NO SPEECH SHOULD LAST MORE THAN TWENTY MINUTES.'

She meant it. She put it in caps.

* I guess 'simple human physics' is biology, right? Biologists gonna hate me.

‘When I gave readings from a book on “awkwardness”, I used to build a performative silence into my opening remarks. When you do this, at first people think that you’re having a breakdown and act alarmed. The silence, which lasts a few beats, feels to the audience like an hour. What you are after, of course, is a breakthrough—a jolt born of disarming quiet to cut through the static and the noise.’

Mary Cappello, in her wonderful book *Lecture*

If you've been tricked into talking for more than twenty minutes the simplest thing is not to fight it. Divide your talk into two twenty-minute chunks. Or three. And put a break in the gaps. The audience might not know it's a break but you do.

Give them a chance to let their minds wander for a couple of minutes, check their phones, whisper to each other, worry whether they've left the gas on.

I often play a video at this point. Something that lasts a couple of minutes. It shifts the energy up or down and gives me a chance to have a break myself. Or you can give the audience some private workshop-y task to do, or maybe you'll do some audience interaction.

The important thing is you're actively managing their attention. That should be the backbone of how you structure and plan a longer presentation.

Then you have to make sure you get their attention back again after the break. This is a good time to ask questions. Or introduce a prop, or a new slide style. Make it clear, hey, it's time to get back on the bus. The simplest way is just to say that. Tell people what you're doing. That works surprisingly well.

If you're a little more confident the most fun – and challenging – thing to do is just pause...

Just stand on the stage and say nothing.
It will feel like an eternity. You won't know what to do with your hands. Don't worry about it. Just stand there.

One by one, and then suddenly and all together, they'll shut up and look at you expectantly.

Now they are yours.

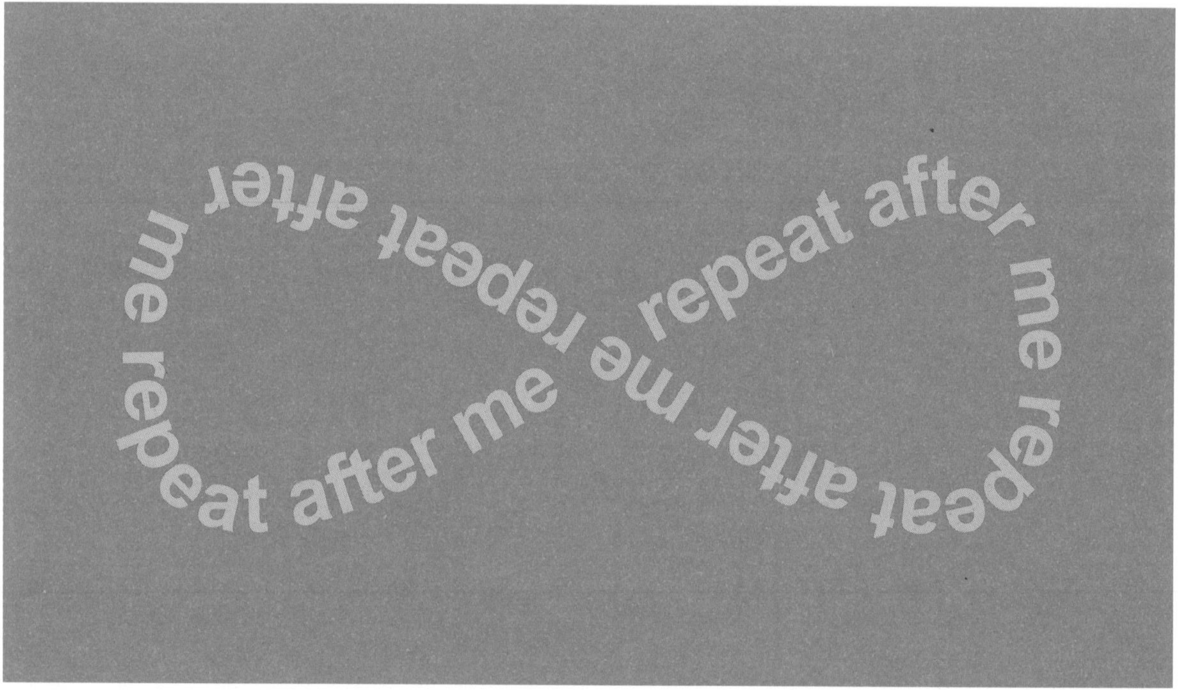
repeat after me repeat after me repeat after me repeat after me

Repeating yourself is difficult but essential

Saying something, and then just saying the same thing again, is tricky. It feels stagy. Hammy. Like you're some sort of orator or salesperson. But it's tremendously effective.

There's no better way of drawing attention to something, of making it clear that this is the important thing, that you're not messing about.

Jon Favreau was head of speechwriting for Barack Obama. He talked to Derek Thompson about the magic of repetition for Thompson's book *Hit Makers*:

> A good line in a speech is like a good piece of music … if you take a small thing and repeat it throughout the speech, like a chorus in a song, it becomes memorable. People don't remember songs for the verses. They remember songs for the chorus. If you want to make something memorable, you have to repeat it.

Thompson heard something similar from musicologist David Huron:

> People find things more pleasurable the more times you repeat them, unless they become aware that you're being repetitive … People want to say, 'I'm not seduced by repetition! I like new things!' But disguised repetition is reliably pleasurable, because it leads to fluency, and fluency makes you feel good.

That's what you're after. Disguised repetition.

Make the same point in lots of different ways

Disguised repetition is also a good way to think about your content. Don't make too many points. Just make the same point in lots of different ways. Use some data, then use an analogy, then use a diagram, then tell a personal story.

Think of your presentation as Velcro.

Velcro doesn't work because it has one big hook like a fishing rod. That's a high-risk strategy. Either that hook works or it doesn't. Velcro works because it has loads of hooks; only some of them need to catch.

You don't know whether your audience members are visual thinkers or like metaphors or just happened to be checking their phone when you made your big important point. Chuck lots of hooks at them. You're more likely to get them.

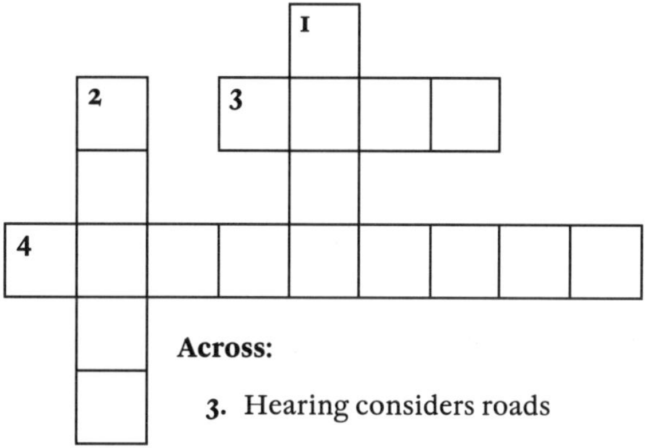

Across:

3. Hearing considers roads
4. Ten riffed in jam for something new

Down:

1. Unchanged American uncle evolves initially
2. People of ignorance not taste primarily gesture

Rhythm
is a dancer

💃

One of your other tools for playing with attention is rhythm. Varying the pace of your slides – and the amount of content on them – helps you keep people awake and helps you make your point.

I had a boss who was a master at this. He'd want to make a point about the amount of stuff his team had made. The normal way to do this is to make a long bulleted list of achievements and then run through the whole list. It soon gets boring, because everyone can read faster than you can talk and what's supposed to be a celebration of achievement turns into a tedious exposition of dull things.

My boss would do it differently. He'd put each of the Twenty Things on a separate slide and just punch through them, one after the other, starting with a bit of an explanation of what the thing was but soon dropping that and just reading it out.

The text was massive, the subtext was clear. We've done THIS and we've done THIS and THIS and THIS.

He would speed up considerably towards the end of the list (which helped to hide the fact that many of the achievements shown there weren't that consequential) and then pause on a big 'HOW ABOUT THAT?' at the end.

On a good day he could wring a round of applause out of a bunch of cynical civil servants. It was a lot to do with rhythm. It had a climactic tempo. It precipitated applause.

(This is another reason why I hate slide transitions. And remote controls. They steal from your rhythm. The timing of a slide is as delicate as the timing of a joke or a drum beat. You don't want any latency ruining it. Bang the space bar – boom – slide.)

It's a well-known hack in journalism that you can make your writing interesting simply by alternating short and long sentences. It sounds silly but it works. Rock bands and musicians have uncovered a similar aesthetic recipe, using extreme variances in volume to enliven otherwise dull rock plods. The Pixies were great at it. So much so that the 2006 documentary made about their comeback tour was titled *loudQUIETloud*.

That says it all. Loud becomes much Louder if juxtaposed with Quiet and Quiet becomes more meaningful when it's more deliberate and not just an absence of shouting.

This works for slides too.

Try making your slides go Lots of Words, Not Many Words, Lots of Words. Or Busy, Empty, Busy. Or Picture, Text, Picture.

For example:

Here's a sequence of slides from Ella Fitzsimmons bringing lots of things together. She's showing the people behind the presentation (that's a bunch of the GDS/Doing Presentations team there), she's treating a slide as a poster, she's got a nice grey background so the slide won't be too glare-y.

But, crucially, look at the rhythm – a big image with a big headline, then a poster-like thing, then a list. Your involvement with each slide changes, you move in and out.

And the presenter gets to do the same. To vary their pace. Sometimes they can let the slide do most of the work. Other times it's down to them.

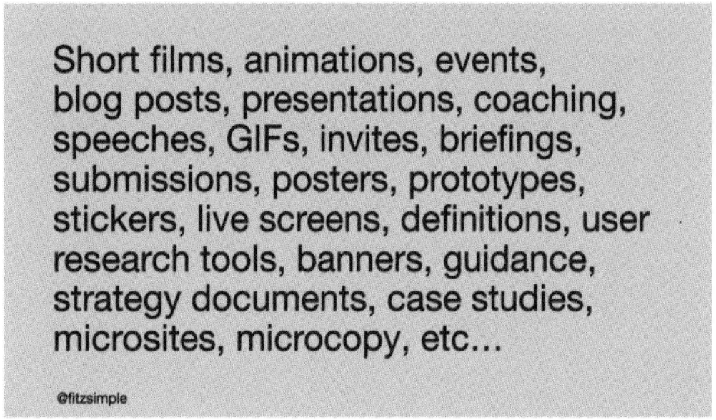

Talk to

everyone

in the room

Don't *just* read the slide

One of the first bits of advice given about presentations is 'don't read the slides'. I've done it myself. This is because a common presentation problem is people writing a lot of stuff on their slides and then just reading it out. This is difficult to watch and pointless.

HOWEVER this is not helpful advice if there are people in the audience who have trouble reading the slides. And there always are.

You have to help those people out. You have to tell them what the slides say. That should be easy if your slides are big, short and readable. But don't just do that.

Speak reasonably slowly. Nervousness makes people speed up. Try not to do that.

Describe the images you're showing on your slides, especially if they're important to your story. And if they aren't important, why are they there?

Explain what your graphs and charts show – which you're doing anyway? Right?

Make sure people can see you and your face, that you're facing the audience and that you're well lit. People will be reading your lips and interpreting your gestures.

If you're working with an interpreter (including a sign language interpreter) leave a bit more of a gap between slides so they can translate the slide before they start translating you. Give them your slides beforehand (and notes or text if you have it). If they've got time, talk them through what you're going to say.

If you show a video, explain what's going on and why you're showing it. Make sure it's got captions. And have some handouts ready for people. Big, easy to read, like your slides. And have something on a USB stick or similar for someone who might want to use a screen reader.

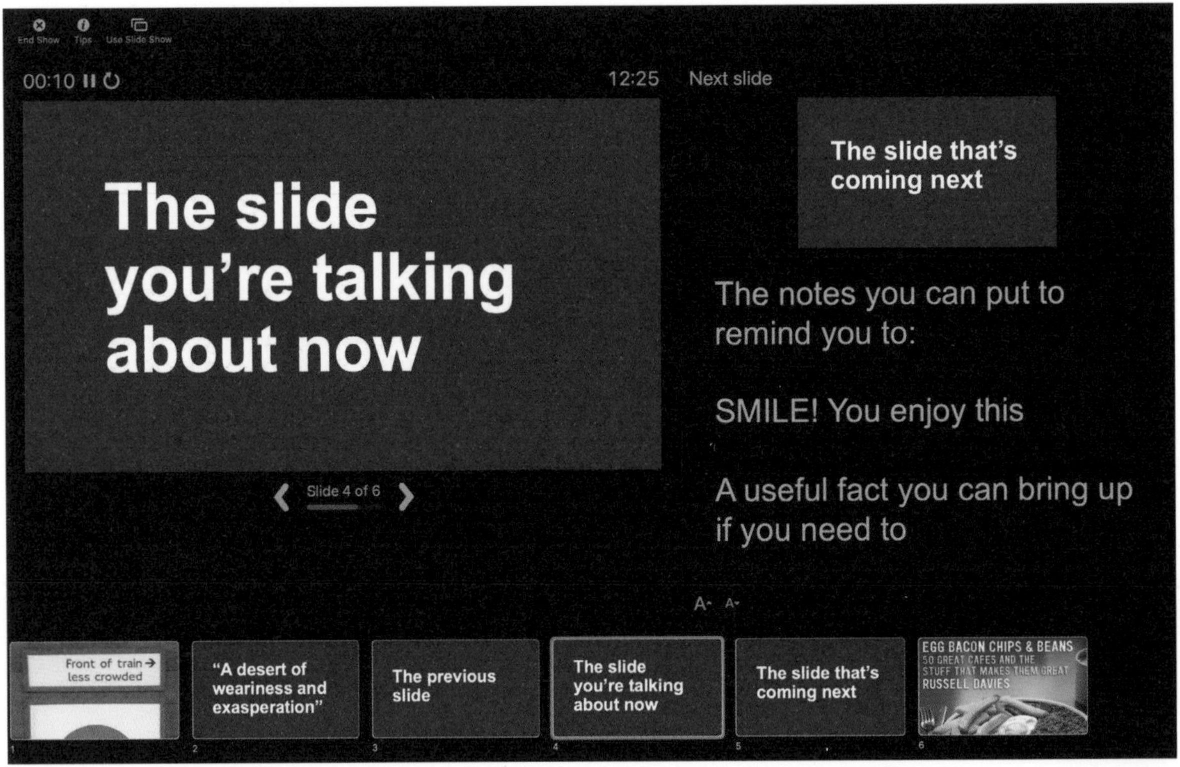
End Show
Tips
Use Slide Show
00:10
12:25
Next slide
The slide you're talking about now
The slide that's coming next
The notes you can put to remind you to:
SMILE! You enjoy this
A useful fact you can bring up if you need to
Slide 4 of 6
Front of train → less crowded
"A desert of weariness and exasperation"
The previous slide
The slide you're talking about now
The slide that's coming next
EGG BACON CHIPS & BEANS
50 GREAT CAFES AND THE STUFF THAT MAKES THEM GREAT
RUSSELL DAVIES
1
2
3
4
5
6

Practically, though...

I'm always surprised when people don't know about Presenter View.

So I'm going to mention it here, just in case.

Presenter View (called slightly different things in other applications, but you'll find it) lets you see something different on your screen to what the audience are seeing on the big screen. You can set it up in a few different ways but I've found the best version is divided into three bits.

The slide the audience can see, the slide that's coming next, your notes.

This makes presenting much easier, especially the 'next slide' feature. It's like you can see into the future. You know where you're going, you can steer your words towards it. (And it means you don't have to be quite as well rehearsed.) Frequent presenters have slide sequences that they do a lot – like a comedian's 'bit' – and they assemble their presentations out of these pre-made sequences. Presenter View's 'next slide' is how they make these transitions feel seamless.

Notes is also useful – but I'd advise using it tactically and sparingly. Don't write down everything you're going to say (at least not in the final version). You don't want to be reading your notes out live. Instead, use the notes as reminders and security. If there's a particular fact you want to be sure of saying, write it there, nice and big. And add instructions to yourself. I write SLOW DOWN every now and then in my notes. And DON'T BE SO MISERABLE.

(Having access to Presenter View is one reason I'm militant about having my laptop onstage with me when I'm doing a big presentation, and actually driving the presentation from it. For a long time conference organisers hated this and didn't understand it. They always thought the monitors they provided at the front of the stage were enough, but they only showed what the audience could see, not Presenter View. This is slowly improving but it's something you have to watch out for.)

Always start the same way
Always start the same way
Always start the same way
Always start the same way
Always start the same way
Always start the same way
Always start the same way
Always start the same way

The most important part of a presentation for you is the beginning. It's when you're the most nervous and the audience is deciding what they think of you. The easiest approach is just to always start the same way. Find a good generic opening that works for you and do it as often as you can.

Advantages: you'll get good at it. You'll know how it works. You'll get more confident, and the audience will sense that confidence and your presentation will go better, giving you even more confidence next time. It's a lovely positive feedback loop.

The best start is probably something about you, a way of introducing yourself. Ideally it would also be unexpected and interesting. Something that makes people lean forward, something they've not heard before.

I always start with a black screen and then I play the 20th Century Fox fanfare. Just standing, looking at the audience, not doing anything. Then the fanfare finishes and I just say, gently and mildly, 'Hello'.

There's normally a laugh at the contrast between the big fanfare and the little hello. And then I say, 'I saw the guy who invented THX sound present once and he started like that. And I thought – all presentations must start like that from now on.' That normally gets a little laugh too. And I mean little. But it's a good laugh, a laugh of relaxation. It's the laugh of some people who've recognised that this talk will contain jokes and be delivered by a human.

And then I just get on with the talk. This isn't the most brilliant opening ever. It's not exactly original (as I point out, I literally stole it from Tomlinson Holman, the THX guy) but I've been doing it for years and it seems to work.

For example:

Nat Buckley is a designer and developer and is fantastic at giving talks. These four slides are the opening to a talk they gave about starting your own company. What a great way to start. An introduction. A joke. A way into the topic and some insight about what kind of person Nat is. Absolutely perfect.

This could be the start of any presentation.

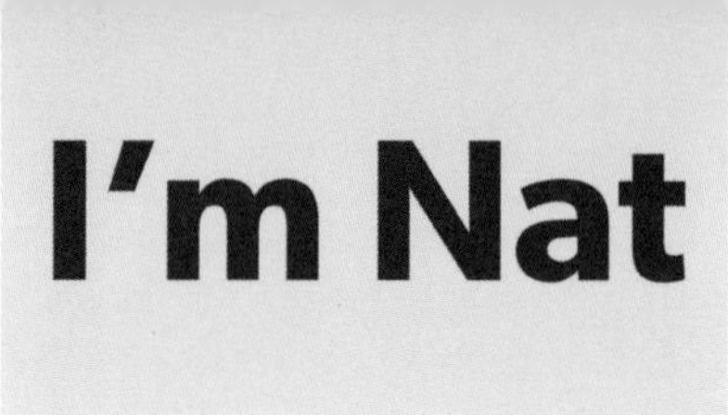
I'm Nat

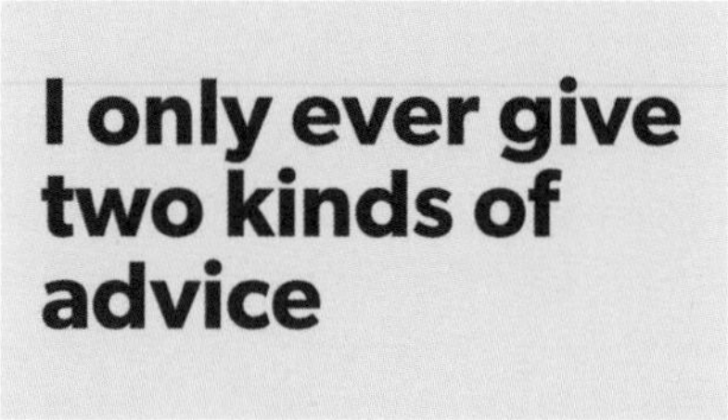
I only ever give two kinds of advice

"Dump him"

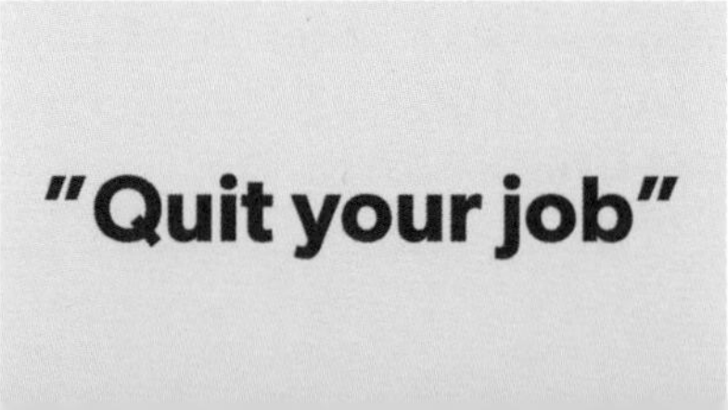
"Quit your job"

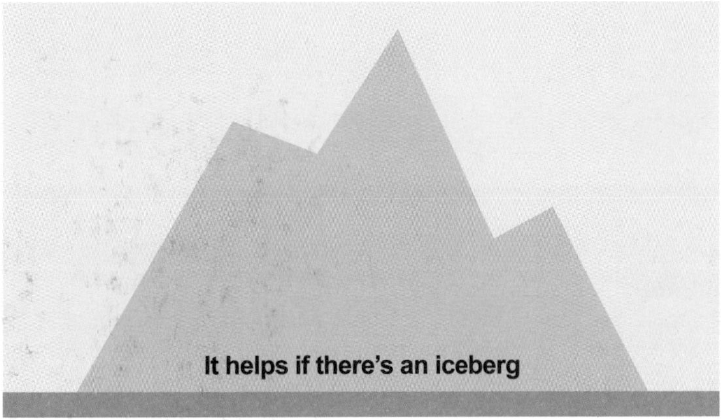
It helps if there's an iceberg

On the campaign trail in 2019, Kamala Harris was asked what made her such a good public speaker. She said this:

> So if you were on the *Titanic*, right, and you know the ship is about to sink and you're the only one who knows – are you going to worry about how you look and how you sound? No, because the thing that's most important is that everyone knows what you know.

Above all, the thing that makes your performance and delivery easy is if you have something important to say. It doesn't have to be the most important thing ever – it probably won't be. But if it's important to you and to someone that you're talking to, that will see you through.

And if it's not important, that's OK too. Have fun and finish early.

THE END

Three ways to have a good ending:

Do it earlier than expected. Nothing garners more joy, respect and gratitude than finishing a presentation early. Everyone will love you. And don't worry too much about building up to the ending. If you've said what needs to be said, just sum it up and declare yourself done.

Sum up. I've always found endings difficult but a few years ago I developed an infallible technique for hiding that fact. When I'm done with my ramblings I say, 'Let's sum up,' and play a video that features quick flashes of every slide from my presentation, in order, with a nice energetic piece of music. People are initially a little taken aback but then they get it. And it's quite useful. They're reminded of the slides and thoughts they've already seen and the music gees everything up a little just when they thought they were on the long, slow slope down to the end.

Get them to clap. And then I bow a little (it's probably more of shrug), put a big THANK YOU on the screen, say, 'That's it,' and get them to clap. This is surprisingly easy to do – people are predisposed to follow clapping cues. And I think it makes a difference. It's a well-known psychological fact that we do not decide to do things and then do them. We do things and then our unconscious mind tricks us into thinking that's what we'd been planning all along. We are not the drivers of our bodies – we are the passengers.

If people clap a lot then that makes them think they've enjoyed something. So get them to clap.

If you're introducing guest speakers get them clapped on as well as off. Americans do this spontaneously; other nations, not so much. And get an audience to clap themselves every now and then. For guessing the answer to something. Or just for sitting there for twenty minutes. You can even tell them why you're doing it. Knowledge of this manipulation doesn't appear to reduce its efficacy.

So let's sum up…

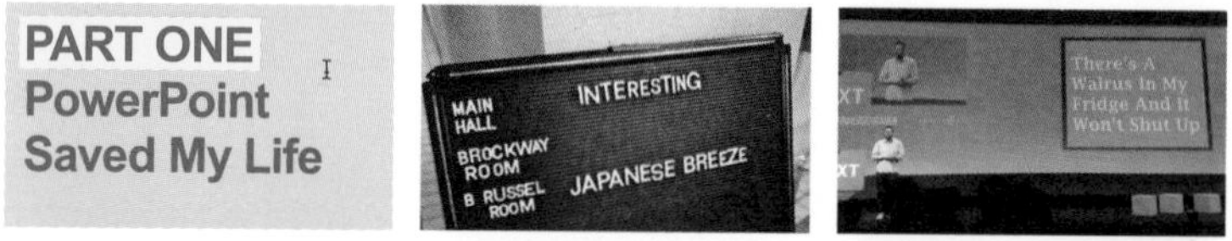
PART ONE
PowerPoint
Saved My Life
MAIN HALL
INTERESTING
BROCKWAY ROOM
B RUSSEL ROOM
JAPANESE BREEZE
There's A
Walrus In My
Fridge And It
Won't Shut Up

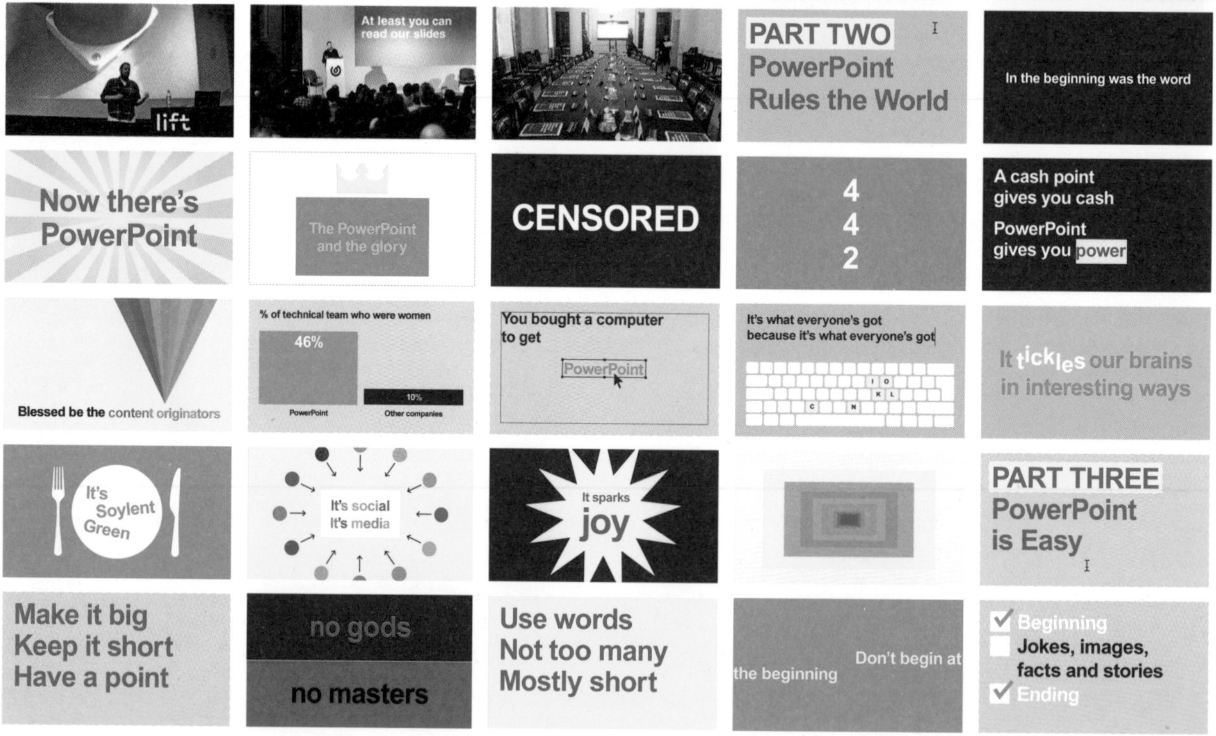
lift
At least you can
read our slides
PART TWO
PowerPoint
Rules the World
In the beginning was the word
Now there's
PowerPoint
The PowerPoint
and the glory
CENSORED
4
4
2
A cash point
gives you cash
PowerPoint
gives you power
Blessed be the content originators
% of technical team who were women
46%
10%
PowerPoint
Other companies
You bought a computer
to get
PowerPoint
It's what everyone's got
because it's what everyone's got
It tickles our brains
in interesting ways
It's
Soylent
Green
It's social
It's media
It sparks
joy
PART THREE
PowerPoint
is Easy
Make it big
Keep it short
Have a point
no gods
no masters
Use words
Not too many
Mostly short
Don't begin at
the beginning
Beginning
Jokes, images,
facts and stories
Ending

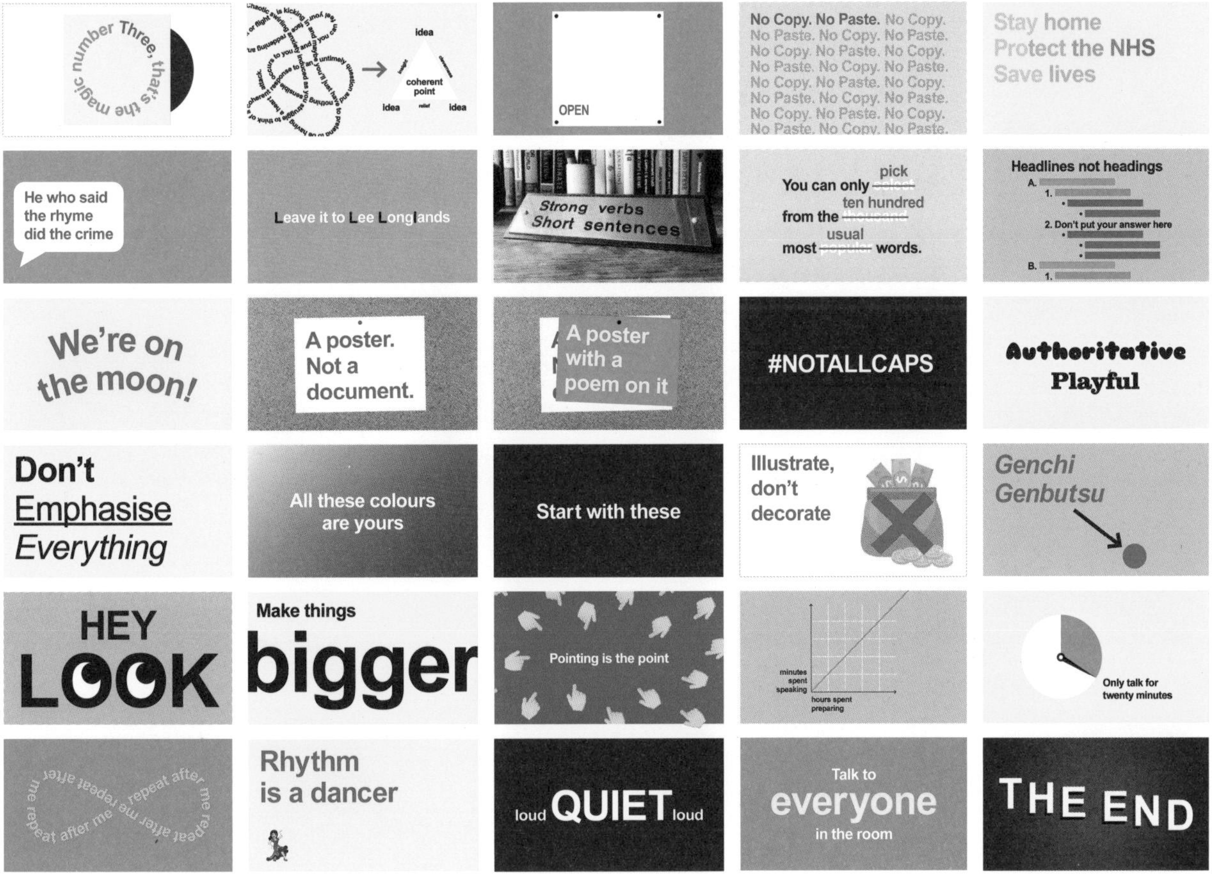
number Three, that's the magic
idea
coherent point
idea
idea
OPEN
No Copy. No Paste. No Copy.
No Paste. No Copy. No Paste.
No Copy. No Paste. No Copy.
No Paste. No Copy. No Paste.
No Copy. No Paste. No Copy.
No Paste. No Copy. No Paste.
No Copy. No Paste. No Copy.
No Paste. No Copy. No Paste.
Stay home
Protect the NHS
Save lives
He who said the rhyme did the crime
Leave it to Lee Longlands
Strong verbs
Short sentences
You can only ~~select~~ pick from the ~~thousand~~ ten hundred most ~~popular~~ usual words.
Headlines not headings
A.
1.
2. Don't put your answer here
B.
1.
We're on the moon!
A poster. Not a document.
A poster with a poem on it
#NOTALLCAPS
Authoritative
Playful
Don't
Emphasise
Everything
All these colours are yours
Start with these
Illustrate, don't decorate
Genchi Genbutsu
HEY LOOK
Make things
bigger
Pointing is the point
minutes spent speaking
hours spent preparing
Only talk for twenty minutes
repeat after me repeat after me
Rhythm is a dancer
loud QUIET loud
Talk to everyone in the room
THE END

BA

NG

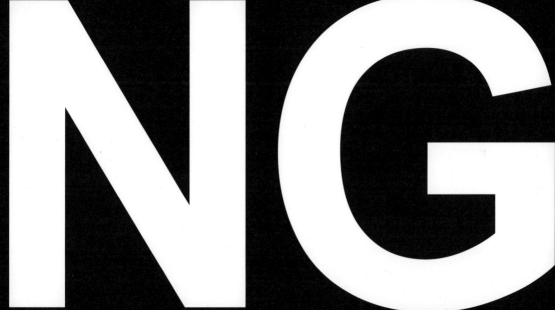

Thank you.
That’s the end.
We ended with a bang.

Please give yourself
a round of applause.

Please make your way to the exits

When you're doing a presentation it's easy to finish early. You're supposed to take forty minutes, so you take thirty-five. Everyone's happy.

With a book it's harder. I wanted to finish early but doing that would have left you with a load of blank pages which would have been mean. (I thought about pretending they were for 'notes' but, really, who does that?)

This is 'the end' but instead of blank pages we've filled it with all sorts of strange miscellanea which wouldn't fit anywhere else.

If I'd just done a presentation and you'd come up afterwards to ask a question (and I hadn't run away and hid in my hotel room), this is the stuff I'd show you. It's a bonus. It's extra. And, to be honest, this stuff is the real gold.

These are my odd theories about PowerPoint that I'd only share if we'd got to know each other a bit.

Three other ways to use PowerPoint:

1. Use it to collect yourself.
2. Use it to bump ideas into each other.
3. Use it in a mysterious third way, which I will not reveal at this point.

1.

Use it to collect yourself

The PowerPoint of the Long You

At some point it will dawn on you that you've been making PowerPoint for your whole career. Probably, if you're under forty, your whole life. As mentioned, PowerPoint is astoundingly backwards compatible, and this provides a joyous opportunity to see it as a companion for life. It will be with you in a way that very little of the modern world will be. Your games consoles will stop loading the games you want to play. Your football team will abandon their stadium and their club colours. Your phone won't last. Neither will your political party. Any professional knowledge you acquire will be made obsolete by AI.

But every PowerPoint file you make will still open. And, splendidly, this turns out to be exactly what you need.

Because you live and work in a world of ideas. And it's only going to get more idea-y. The drudgery's going to get automated, farmed out to the learning machines. If you want to get paid in twenty years' time you're going to have to be having ideas. Good ones. And wouldn't it be nice to have a tool to help you?

But then you have to worry – what should I collect? What would be useful?

It's simple. Things that interest you. Things you find fascinating. Remember – this is a long-term pursuit, there's not much point trying to guess what's going to be useful or career-enhancing ten or fifteen years from now. Instead you should have faith that what interests you is going to come in handy. Because it almost certainly will.

And if it doesn't interest you you're not going to do it diligently and it's going to feel like work.

Make your natural inquisitiveness into something a little more structured. Turn it from idly browsing the internet into research.

The American writer and anthropologist Zora Neale Hurston put it well:

> Research is formalized curiosity. It is poking and prying with a purpose.

It also forces you to ask yourself a useful question: what, deep down, am I interested in? It's not something we're often asked. I've raised it in many training sessions and people find it hard to answer. Quite a lot of the answers people give are the generic things you get at the end of CVs: film, walking, literature. Fine, but digging into those things and going a bit further to find out what actually lights you up is a useful exercise.

As Baudrillard said: 'What you really collect is always yourself.'*

Having a place where you can noodle, collect and play around when your energy is low means you can add to your thinking when you're short of inspiration. You can persist with things without having to get fired up to do them.

* This is very PowerPoint. Just sticking a quote in like this. I know absolutely nothing about Baudrillard. I'm guessing French? A man? Probably the author of impenetrable philosophy? I just came across this quote and I love it. I know, I know. It's not a million miles from having 'Every Breath You Take' played at your wedding. I'm so superficial.

> I go to my studio every day. Some days the work comes easily. Other days nothing happens. Yet on the good days the inspiration is only an accumulation of all the other days, the non-productive ones.
>
> Beverly Pepper

That's the kind of work that will give you a long-term advantage. It's like the compound interest of ideas, you pay in a small amount every week and suddenly, five years later, you've got everything you need to write a book.

You may have noticed, for instance, that I have a long-term interest in people who've had long-term interests in how ideas come from having long-term interests in things.

> There's a point, around the age of twenty, when you have to choose whether to be like everybody else the rest of your life, or to make a virtue of your peculiarities.
>
> Bedap of Anarres in Ursula K. Le Guin's *The Dispossessed*

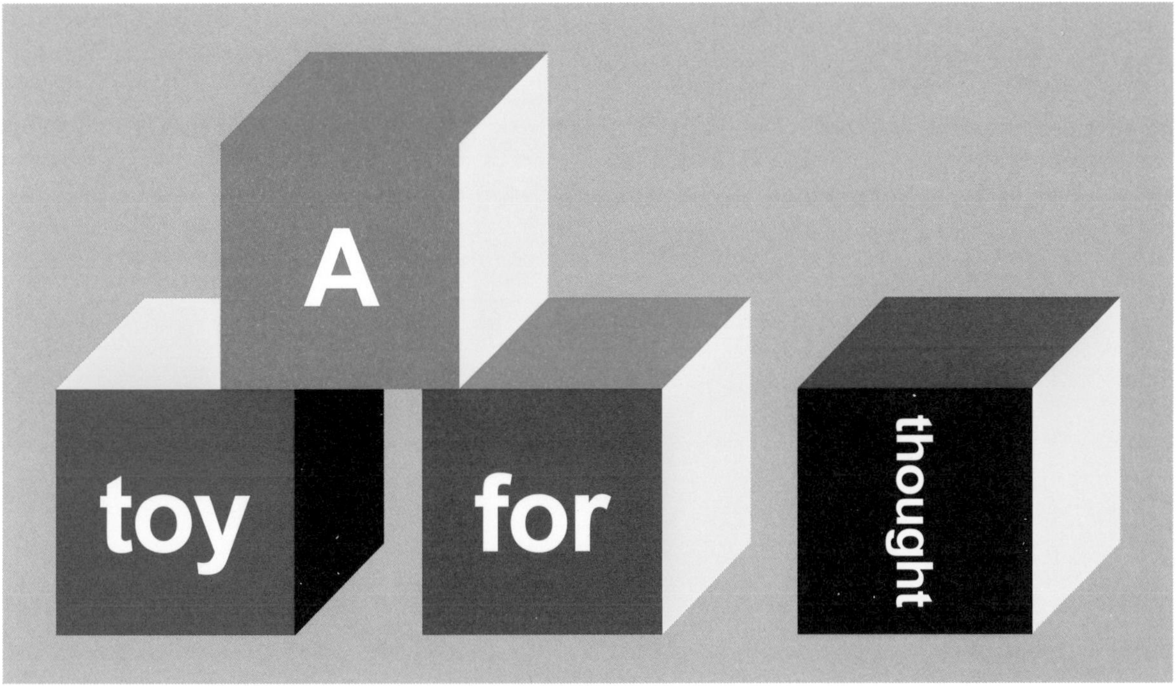
A
toy
for
thought

I read books and articles about this stuff, which lead me to other books and articles and furnish me with tremendous quotes and citations. And then I can just quote other people and you realise it's not just me saying it.

I could, for example, add something in here about how it's useful to make this a regular practice, to make a habit of it. Or I could leave it to Octavia E. Butler:

> First forget inspiration. Habit is more dependable. Habit will sustain you whether you're inspired or not. Habit will help you finish and polish your stories. Inspiration won't. Habit is persistence in practice.

Cathy Marshall of Xerox PARC described her hypertext systems as 'idea processors'. That's what you should do with your deck. Put quotes next to each other, juxtapose them with images, find a pithy way to summarise an article you've just read. Put a better headline on it. Find out what you think about things by making slides and slide sequences.

Writing in fragments and thoughts like this is so much easier, and potentially more useful, than trying to think in paragraphs or presentations – they can come later.

Another Xerox PARC alum called Rich Gold wrote a lovely, strange little book called *The Plenitude*. In it he describes PowerPoint as 'a toy for thought'. That's always been my favourite description of what it can do, of why it's more than corporate droneware, and so liberating, creative and fun.

Practically, though…

Make yourself a blank PowerPoint deck. When you've done a presentation put all your slides in it. Remove the boring slides. Keep the ones that worked. When you find an interesting quote or image, stick it on a slide and add it to the deck. Took an interesting photo? Do the same. If you have a little thought about something – pop it in the deck. If you've got five minutes – try to find an image to illustrate that thought. Or if you started with an image – spend five minutes wondering what idea it might illustrate. Experiment with colours. With fonts. With bits of music and video.

It's a scrapbook. A multimedia scrapbook. That's all. But start it now. Future You will be so proud of Present You. This is the work you can do when real thinking seems too hard. It's like grinding in a video game. Not a Big Boss Battle but satisfying in its own way and useful. You scroll around the world looking for material and popping it in your deck.

This is a thing that professionally creative people do. They snap up things that catch their eye, they may not know why, but they'll paste them in and keep them for later. Then, when they're lost and aimless, looking for ideas, they'll open up their scrapbooks and browse around. Sooner or later that little sparkle of something that didn't make sense before, in collision with the thing on the next page, is exactly what they're looking for.

And, as Katharine Hepburn said, 'If you always do what interests you, at least one person is pleased.'

2.

Use it

to bump

ideas

into

each

other

> I write entirely to find out what I'm thinking.
>
> Joan Didion

That's why you're collecting.

To make your thinking easier and more personal.

It's becoming clear to the people who study these things that the best ideas aren't flashes of inspiration, they're the result of a long and diligent pursuit of one field of study cross-pollinated with another. Ideas are built from slow hunches, they're noodled with over time, accreted from interests and obsessions.

As the writer Steven Johnson puts it, in an article in the *Wall Street Journal*:

> …ideas are works of bricolage. They are, almost inevitably, networks of other ideas. We take the ideas we've inherited or stumbled across, and we jigger them together into some new shape. We like to think of our ideas as a $40,000 incubator, shipped direct from the factory, but in reality they've been cobbled together with spare parts that happened to be sitting in the garage.

The people who have the most and the best ideas are interested in lots of different things, they follow those trails of thought, and they have ways to collect those pursuits and smash them into each other.

PowerPoint is brilliant for this because it's so absorbent. It can soak up text, images, video and music and it will show them all to you full-screen.

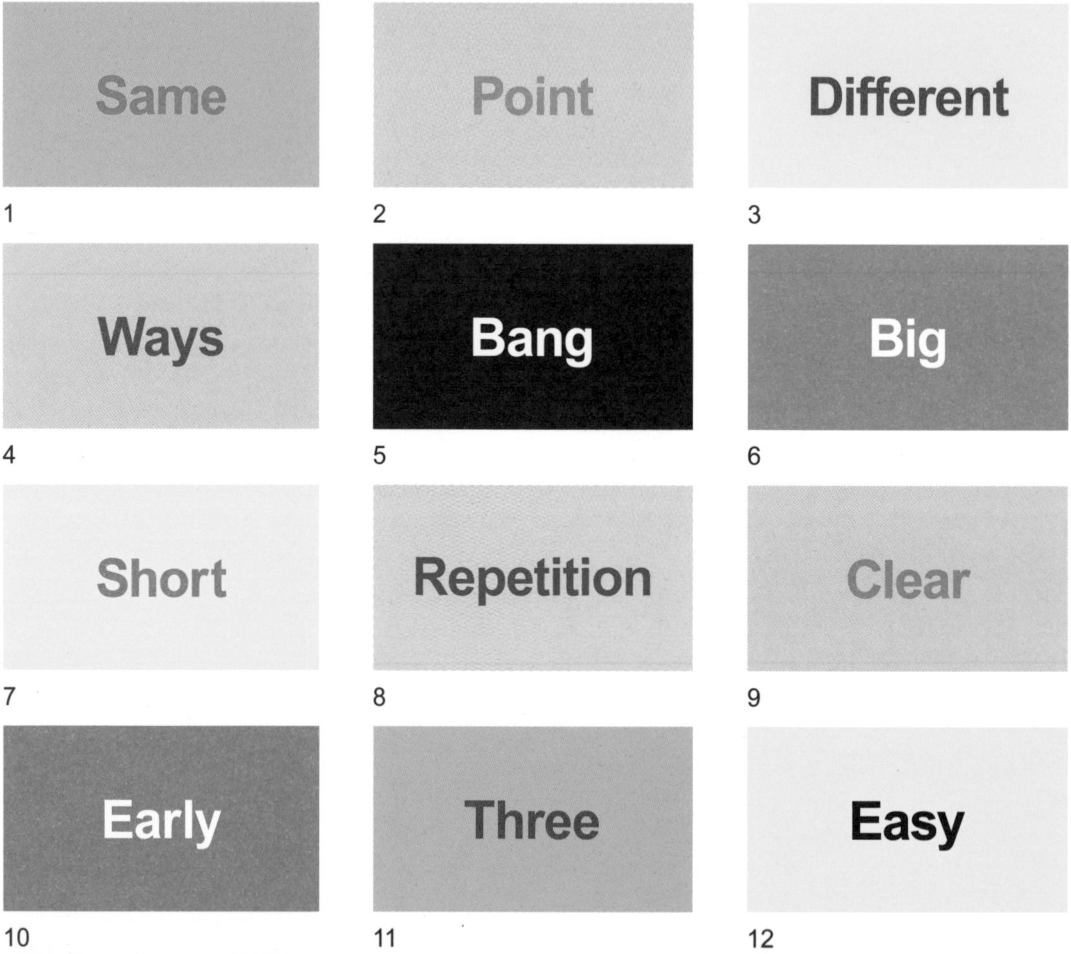
Same
1
Point
2
Different
3
Ways
4
Bang
5
Big
6
Short
7
Repetition
8
Clear
9
Early
10
Three
11
Easy
12

Now, when you're writing a presentation you're not starting from scratch. You're not going into a room with bare walls and blank piece of paper.

You're starting with a ton of notes, surrounded by inspiration. Engage Slide Sorter. Flip through your deck. Find the bits that might be relevant to your task. Move them around. Bump ideas into each other. Those collisions will give you new ideas and make you realise new things.

Stick some blank slides in places where you know you'll need something. Suddenly you don't need to write a presentation – you've got a third of it already, you just need some more slides.

Then think of yourself as Anna Wintour.

Watch *The September Issue*, the documentary that shows her putting together an issue of *Vogue* magazine. You'll see that throughout the movie she keeps going back to a room where they keep a 'flatplan' of the magazine. It's a wall with little shelves designed to hold tiny printouts of the pages so Anna can see the whole thing spread out in front of her like a Media Deity. It's not a view a normal mortal gets.

That's what Slide Sorter gives you. Your audience will never see your presentation like that. But if you use it well you'll be able to create rhythm and flow in the way a great magazine editor or film director does.

(By the way, if it's a presentation you're collaborating on with a few other people, print it off, get in a room and stick it on the walls. It's such a useful and effective way to get this sort of thing done. You'll see where the weaknesses are straight away. Where it's too long, too flabby, where there's not enough material.)

3.

Use it in a mysterious third way which I will now reveal

There isn't one! It was a trick so I could finish early again.

Always be finishing early.

Acknowledgements

PowerPoint has an uneasy relationship with credits and acknowledgements. It's like hip-hop and sampling. It's powerful because it makes it easy for you to build your own ideas on other people's. And, because most presentations are given to small audiences, you can 'get away with it'.

So try to be especially careful and generous about credit and acknowledgement. The underlying web of connections and ideas is part of what you're presenting. Give people a chance to follow your influences backwards, to find their inspiration where you found yours. Hip-hop is how the world rediscovered hundreds of genius soul artists. Maybe you can be the way someone rediscovers a favourite influence of yours. (And I'm very nervous that I've messed that up, somehow, in here. If I have, I'm very sorry. Please let me know.)

An acknowledgement: my friend Ella Fitzsimmons taught me this.

The list of books, people and presentations that made this book is huge and would mostly be an enormous screed of URLs that you're never going to type into your computer. So I've made a special place where you can find resources that might help and inspire you. It's at www.russelldavies.com/powerpoint.

But here are the Ten Best Books that got me to writing this one. Not all of the influences will be obvious, but they're probably the important ones.

On PowerPoint: *Sweating Bullets: Notes about Inventing PowerPoint* by Robert Gaskins (Vinland, 2012)

On presenting: *slide:ology* by Nancy Duarte (O'Reilly Media, Inc., 2008)

On information and design: everything by Edward Tufte, but especially *The Visual Display of Quantitative Information* (Graphics Press, 1983)

On speaking in public: *Lecture* by Mary Cappello (Transit, 2020)

On how language works: *Because Internet: Understanding the New Rules of Language* by Gretchen McCulloch (Riverhead, 2019)

On life as an introvert: *Quiet: The Power of Introverts in a World That Can't Stop Talking* by Susan Cain (Crown, 2012)

On tech culture and invention: *Broad Band: The Untold Story of the Women Who Made the Internet* by Claire L. Evans (Portfolio, 2018)

On writing: *First You Write a Sentence: The Elements of Reading, Writing … and Life* by Joe Moran (Penguin, 2018)

On writing again: *Write to the Point: How to be Clear, Correct and Persuasive on the Page* by Sam Leith (Profile, 2017)

On life online: *Lurking: How a Person Became a User* by Joanne McNeil (MCD, 2020)

And I need to say thank you

To Anne Shewring for everything and for being the first reader. Flora Joll, Ben Terrett RDI, Clem Hobson, Ella Fitzsimmons and Denise Wilton for being the next readers. Anthony Topping for thinking of the title, making me write the book and not letting me change the title. Helen Conford and Cecily Gayford for always being right and patient at the same time (and Cecily for 'euphoric polychrome'). Lottie Fyfe for making it happen. Nathaniel McKenzie for making it legal. Sam Matthews for proofreading. Rachel, Ella, Nat, Jon and Flora for letting me include their stuff, and Alice Bartlett for the crossword. Noah Brier. Lindsey Keighley and Etienne Pollard for sending me things that I then left out (sorry). Hayden Wood and Lis Blair for the patience and the time off. David Rowan for commissioning the *Wired* piece. To Richard Morton for nudging me politely about accessibility. To the bus drivers of London, who don't get thanked enough. To Arthur Davies for everything else.

To everyone I've ever seen do PowerPoint and stolen something from. Chris Riley, Neil Christie, Trish Adams, John Shaw, Camilla Harrison, Stuart Smith, Matt Boffey, Tony and Kim and everyone at w+k, Nicki Sprinz, Helen Fuchs, James Higgs and everyone at ustwo. Ade Adewunmi, Ali Kelly, Mike Bracken, Tom Loosemore, Mark Hurrell, Etienne Pollard, Lindsey Keighley, Giles Turnbull, Matt Sheret and everyone at GDS. Hayden Wood, Jenny Zhao and everyone at Bulb, Ben Terrett, RDI, Tom Taylor, Anne Ward, Alice Bartlett, Chris Heathcote, Tom Stuart, Toby Barnes, Alexandra Deschamps-Sonsino, Phil Gyford, James Bridle, Matts Webb, Jones, Ward, Locke and Irvine Brown, Jack Schulze, Kevin Slavin, Beeker Northam, Martha Lane Fox, Dave Hieatt, Tomlinson Holman and everyone who ever spoke at Interesting. Collectively to the DoingPresentations crew, the BRIG alumni, THFT, the RSS massive, BLB MKTNG and to Team Coffee Morning.

To the *Rule of Three* and *In Writing with Hattie Crisell* podcasts for inspiration.

To Clem and Jenny: *curre ad arma.*

To Robert Gaskins for inventing PowerPoint.

And to Stefanie Posavec for designing this thing in the most difficult of circumstances (COVID, me). Anything good about this book is because of Stef. Buy her books.

Image credits

Images on the following pages are historical PowerPoint screenshots: 7, 8, 9, 11, 13, 18; images on the following pages are courtesy of the author: 124, 150, 152, 160, 189, 232; p. 15 © Chris Heathcote; p. 17 © Erno Hannink, via Creative Commons licence (CC BY 2.0); p. 20 © Stephanie Booth; p. 23 © Manox Media / Future Everything; p. 24 © Ali Kelly; p. 39 source: US Department of State Archive, https://2001-2009.state.gov/secretary/former/powell/remarks/2003/17300.htm; p. 40 © E. B. Tait; p. 42 source: NSA document leaked by Edward Snowden and published in the *Washington Post* ('NSA infiltrates links to Yahoo, Google data centers worldwide, Snowden documents say'),

30 October 2013; p. 44 © CBS Photo Archive / Getty Images; p. 46 source: The Marshall Project, https://www.themarshallproject.org/2014/12/23/powerpoint-justice, photo illustration by Lisa Iaboni; p. 49 source: The New School/Shannon Mattern via YouTube, https://www.youtube.com/watch?v=HzhC3BIH1a4; p. 50 © PA Images / Alamy Stock Photo; p. 54 Image from Envisioning Emotional Epistemological Information by David Byrne. Copyright © 2003 by Todo Mundo Ltd., used by permission of The Wylie Agency LLC; p. 55 *Protect Protect*, 2007. Oil on linen, 79 × 102.25 in. / 200.7 x 259.7 cm. Text: U.S. government document. © Jenny Holzer. ARS, NY and DACS, London 2021; pp. 56–60 © SoftBank; p. 64 source: Joint Air Power Competence Centre, https://news.usni.org/2020/10/27/report-to-congress-on-joint-all-domain-command-and-control; p. 66 source: Army Research, Development and Engineering Command; p. 67 source: US Army 1st Sustainment Brigade Sustainment Operations Center; p. 68 sources: top left US military; top right 2020 Update of the SEBoK Context Diagram (SEBoK Original) created by Ifezue Obiako; bottom left British Army/MoD; bottom right: Defense Information Systems Agency; p. 69 source: 'What is the DoDAF Meta Model (DM2)?', US Department of Defense; p. 70 source: Air Force Global Strike Command; p. 71 source: US military; p. 76–7 © Jennifer Egan, first published in *A Message from the Goon Squad*, 2011; p. 94 permission granted by copyright holders; p. 135 © Flora Joll; p. 149 source: YouTube pitch deck disclosed as part of a deposition in a court case between Viacom and YouTube (Google) in 2010, https://www.alexanderjarvis.com/youtube-seed-stage-startup-pitch-deck/; p. 185 © Svetlana Borokh / Alamy Stock Vector; p. 187 © Rachel Coldicutt; p. 190 Owais Raza via Twitter (@reye27); p. 194 © CERN; p. 199 courtesy of Jon Steel, from his book *Perfect Pitch: The Art of Selling Ideas and Winning New Business*; p. 224 Andrew Kitching / Alamy Stock Photo; p. 229 courtesy of Ella Fitzsimmons.

The Pedant's Prayer or Hypocritic Oath

Lord, forgive me for I live in a glass house and
am with sin, yet I both throw and cast stones.
I find fault but I am faulty.
I nitpick but I am a nitwit.
I poke holes but I am not holy.
And the apostrophe on Pedant's is probably
in the wrong place.
Any mistakes, misattributions, omissions
or hypocrisies are mine.
We regret the error.

Environmental statement

We're in the middle of a climate crisis. Publishing a book has a carbon impact. Most of the carbon impact for something like this is in the printing (in China) and shipping (by boat). There is obviously some from the amount of time we've spent on Zoom calls and googling military PowerPoint but it's the printing and paper that's the big thing. So we're going to offset that to try and pay something back to the planet. The offsets are organised and audited by my friends at Bulb. They're legit. They pay for rainforest to be protected and for renewables projects, which otherwise wouldn't have happened, to be built.

I asked Profile to come up with the CO_2 impact of each book but they couldn't really figure it out. It's not easy and it'll depend on how many copies end up being printed etc. In *How Bad Are Bananas?* (Profile Books, 2010) Mike Berners-Lee suggests a high-end paperback with virgin paper has an impact of around 2kg CO_2e, so I'm going to account for 3kg CO_2e per copy for this book. When we're able to be more precise about the impact we'll update that if we need to.

Please consider visiting www.bulb.co.uk/carbon-calculator and doing some offsetting of your own.

Thank you.

Next slide please.